JOURNEY
OF THE
BIBLE

JOURNEY
OF THE
BIBLE

THE REMARKABLE

STORY OF HOW

THE BIBLE

CAME FROM GOD

TO YOU

■

Irving L. Jensen

World Wide Publications
Minneapolis, Minnesota 55403

Journey of the Bible

© 1990 Irving L. Jensen

World Wide Publications is the publishing ministry of the Billy Graham Evangelistic Association.

Unless otherwise noted, Scripture quotations are taken from The Everyday Bible, New Century Version. Copyright © 1987 by Worthy Publishing, Fort Worth, Texas 76137. Used by permission.

Scripture quotations marked NIV are taken from The Holy Bible, New International Version. Copyright © 1973, 1978, 1984 International Bible Society. Used by permission of Zondervan Bible Publishers.

Scripture quotations marked KJV are taken from the Authorized King James Version of the Bible.

Bible verses marked NKJV are taken by permission from The Bible, The New King James Version, copyright © 1979, 1980, 1982 Thomas Nelson, Inc., Thomas Nelson Publishers.

Library of Congress Catalog Card Number: 90-070297

ISBN: 0-89066-192-8

Printed in the United States of America

90 91 92 93 94 / 5 4 3 2 1

Contents

CHARTS

Dedicated to my wife Charlotte
and our children Donna, Karen, and Bob,
who have helped make my joy of writing
about the Bible so full, because they
love the Lord and his Book, too.

Preface

The story of the Bible's journey from God to the world is as exciting as it is interesting. I taught the subject at a college for many years, and each succeeding year left deep impressions with me that keep magnifying God's Book as one matchless miracle. The evidences of the miracle are irrefutable. There is absolutely no other way to regard the Bible.

I hope the chapters of this book will stir in you a growing interest in the action-packed journey of the Bible from God to you. Don't be just a spectator. Keep reminding yourself that *your own heart* is one of the destinations of that age-long journey.

—Irving Jensen
Dayton, Tennessee
May 1990

Introduction

It was a mild spring day, and I had just arrived home from high school. Mom was in the kitchen when the doorbell rang. I was nearest the door, so I went to answer. I didn't know that the next minutes were to begin a new period of my life, centered around the book that had already become my favorite possession—the Bible.

Mom and Pop had always put the Bible first in our home. What precious memories we six children have had of them—Pa reading the Bible at family devotions, and dear Mom working her hardest to get the whole flock off to Sunday school on time.

It was Depression time in America after the Wall Street crash, so we didn't have many material possessions. Each of us had his own copy of the Bible—but didn't everyone in church own a Bible? In our home all of us believed that the Bible was God's holy Word, teaching the gospel message of salvation by faith in Christ. But when I think about those days now, I don't recall ever getting excited or enthused about what the printed pages of the Bible *looked like*. I saw only sameness, tameness, and lameness.

Some of our public school textbooks had very attractive pages. But most Bibles I had seen looked the same: each page had two columns of plain, printed text, with small numbers to indicate new chapters and verses. Some Bibles had headings at the top of each page or at the beginning of each chapter. But that was it. There were no blank spaces to encourage the recording of notes, and there were no outlines or other helps. Even attention words like "Behold" got lost in the sameness of the printed lines. I loved the Bible, and as a young teenager had memorized hundreds of verses, but the "blah" appearance of the printed text didn't excite me or start me off on a Bible study safari.

That's where I was when the doorbell rang. I opened the door and saw a man holding a large, thick book in his hand. He said he was selling a new edition of the Bible that would help people read and study God's Book. I was all ears and eyes—after all, the Bible was my favorite book. As he turned the pages, I could not believe what I was seeing—printed pages that seemed to talk and invite me to spend a lot of time with them. Each page had four columns divided by three vertical lines. The outer columns surrounded the Bible text, and in those columns were study helps, such as lists of key words with numbers attached, references to related verses, clear outlines, and many blank spaces. The salesman also showed me the three-hundred-plus pages of helps at the end of the volume, but I was mainly attracted to the unusual format of the Bible text. This was what I wanted.

When he quoted the down-payment price, I didn't hesitate emptying my "piggy bank." I was so excited I didn't even check with Mom about what I was doing. She knew I had a little coin bank on my dresser, but she didn't know how much was in it. In fact, neither did I. Today I can't recall how, as a teenager, I was able to save money during the Depression—even that was surely a part of God's plan to start me on my new experience in Bible study and my teaching career.

The day the post office delivered my new Bible was a milestone in my life. The Bible had come a long way on its journey, and now a copy of a brand new study Bible was in my hands. From that day on, Bible study would always be exciting and fun, as well as instructive. Today, the soiled and torn pages of the rebound copy remind me of the many hours I spent as a teenager studying the text in my bedroom. I have often thought of the salesman whom God sent to our house to start me on my way to a ministry centered on his Word. I wish I could thank that man for walking the streets of Staten Island in the middle of the Depression, and ringing the doorbell of a small, plain house on Fiske Avenue.

Many Bible Editions

Have you ever shopped in a local Christian bookstore, looking for a Bible? If so, you probably saw very quickly the large variety of choices. Did you want the traditional King James Version or a modern translation? Paraphrase or literal text? Leather-bound or hardcover? Thin or heavy paper? Large or small print? Single or multi-column? In addition, you would have seen different kinds of *study Bibles*—volumes that include helps to study the Bible text. Included among the helps are background and survey information, running outlines of the Bible text, footnote references to related Bible verses, brief explanations and commentaries, and a variety of appendix helps at the end of the volume.

Those are some of the elements that determine which Bible edition we finally choose for personal Bible reading and study. All of us can profit from the excellent helps and incentives for Bible study. But even with a new Bible in our hand, which we plan to read and study conscientiously, few of us ask the question, "How did this Bible get here in the first place?" If we knew the answer, it would enhance our view of Scripture and keep our hearts alert to the tremendous truth that this is indeed a Miracle Book.

Miracle Journey of the Miracle Book

You may have already experienced the miraculous nature of God's Book in terms of its *internal* witness, within your own heart:

> God's word is alive and working. It is sharper than a sword sharpened on both sides. It cuts all the way into us, where the soul and spirit are joined. It cuts to the center of our joints and our bones. And God's word judges the thoughts and feelings in our hearts. (Hebrews 4:12)

The Bible's *external* witness as a Miracle Book is demonstrated by its journey from God to the human race. Anyone who studies this history objectively has to conclude that the Bible is truly a Miracle Book. I can hardly hold the Bible in my hand or see it on my desk, opened to any page, without a feeling of awe and assurance that *this is truly God's voice to me.*

Many honest questions are asked about the Bible's journey from God to us. They themselves show why a study of the journey is such an important exercise. Here are some of the main questions that will be answered in this book:

1. Why did God give the Bible to the world?
2. When were the books of the Old Testament and New Testament written?
3. Does the Bible actually *claim* to be the Word of God? If so, how sound is that claim?
4. How were the human authors selected?
5. Were the original manuscripts perfect, without error? Why is the answer to this question so crucial?

6. Who determined what books would be included in the Old Testament group and in the New Testament?
7. Since we don't have any of the original Bible manuscripts, how confident can we be that the existing copies are true to those originals?
8. What is a "literal" translation? What is a "free" translation?
9. Is something lost from the originals in the process of translation?
10. What is a paraphrased Bible, and how dependable is it?
11. Why are there so many English versions?
12. What is a Study Bible, and what are its values?
13. How can one explain why the Bible remains as the most-read book in the world?

The journey of the Bible from God to us was not a quick, overnight trip. It has spanned several centuries, and the Book has survived countless attacks along the way. The accompanying chart shows six stages of the journey. As you read the following brief descriptions of the stages, observe how each fits into the chart of the journey.

1. *Communication*—God always seeks contact with each person of his creation. He wants to talk to us.

2. *Revelation*—God reveals the truth to all mankind.

3. *Inspiration and composition*—God moves chosen authors to write inspired manuscripts. Thirty-nine manuscripts, written in Hebrew, are of pre-Christian years; and twenty-seven, written in Greek, are after Christ (a few lines of both Testaments are in Aramaic).

4. *Canonization*—By the influence of people of God, who are moved by the Spirit of God, the thirty-nine

Hebrew books gradually merge into one group, now called the Old Testament; and the twenty-seven Greek books merge into the New Testament.

5. *Transmission*—Hand copies of the original manuscripts are made before the autographs (see footnote 3) disappear from public circulation. Then, copies are made of copies in the centuries that follow. From the middle of the fifteenth century A.D., the copies are *printed* copies.

6. *Translation*—The Hebrew Old Testament and Greek New Testament are translated into many languages of the world. Each translated copy reaches its final destination in the hands of a happy owner, to be read and studied.

The last entry on the accompanying chart, covering all the centuries since the first autographs were written, is *preservation*. The word reminds us that the Bible is invincible. The salvation verse of John 3:16 proclaims the same truth in our English Bible as the apostle John wrote it in Greek, nineteen hundred years ago. That is supernatural preservation. Every day, that verse's message of salvation is reaching thousands of new readers. What an exciting, wonderful ministry!

JOURNEY OF THE BIBLE FROM GOD TO YOU

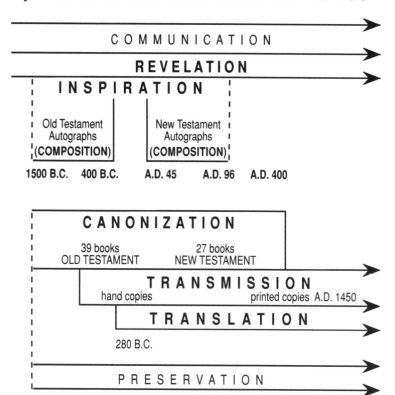

1

Communication and Revelation— God Talks to Us

One of the greatest statements of the Bible is the exclamation, "God has spoken!" (Hebrews 1:2) Over the centuries God has spoken to the world in many different ways, such as through prophets (Hebrews 1:1), teachers (2:1), angels (2:2), miraculous signs (2:4), the Holy Spirit (2:4), and the Scriptures (3:7-11). His highest and greatest communication has been through his beloved Son—Jesus the Creator (Hebrews 1:2), Savior (1:3), and teacher (2:3). The Bible is God's written record of what he has spoken through his Son. It is a message of hope for the entire world: "Because of God's grace, he [Jesus] died for everyone" (Hebrews 2:9).

I. Communication

There was a time in world history when no part of the Bible had yet been written. Adam and Eve didn't have a Bible, nor did Noah or Abraham. If Moses' books (Genesis through Deuteronomy) were the first Scripture to be written, the world didn't have any portion until around

1500 B.C.—at least 1000 to 2000 years after the time of Adam and Eve. (See the chart, JOURNEY OF THE BIBLE FROM GOD TO YOU, page 17.) The question that naturally arises is: Why did God give the Bible to the world in the first place?

Part of the answer involves *communication*. God is love—he loves the world. He has always wanted to have spiritual fellowship with everyone whom he has created. He has initiated fellowship with those who believe, sending messages to them in different ways. And he has had to refuse fellowship with those who reject him (Romans 1:21-28).

In pre-Bible times God spoke with audible words, heard by ear, or by inaudible words, heard by the person's spirit. Often he spoke words through angels, who are his messengers (e.g., Genesis 16:7). His first words to Adam and Eve were words of blessing and encouragement: "Have many children and grow in number" (Genesis 1:28). He gave instructions to Noah for building an ark: "Build a boat of cypress wood" (Genesis 6:14).

We can see how often God spoke to people in Old Testament times by looking through a Bible concordance. The words *said* and *saith*, which refer mostly to God or the Lord, appear almost four thousand times. A similar high count is also true of Jesus' spoken words, recorded in the New Testament.

But God has also communicated with people through things he *did*. He proclaimed judgment to the sinful world by sending a flood (Genesis 7:21). And he demonstrated his mercy and power by remembering Noah and his family and stopping the flood rains (Genesis 8:1-2). To this day, whatever God communicates to man is an important message about who he is (his person) and what he does (his work).

So, God has always communicated with mankind. This leads us back to the original question: Why did God give the Bible to the world?

Another part of the answer to that question has to do with the *message* of the Bible. God has always wanted to tell the whole world the story of salvation from sin and judgment. That story involves a full revelation of himself and his creation, in time and eternity. God knows all things. According to his perfect planning, he chose to broadcast worldwide the message of salvation. He would do this through one long book which he would inspire men to write. It would be translated into the mother tongues of all nations, and would survive until the end of time.

What a book that had to be! It must perfectly reveal God, identify sin and judgment, and show sinners how to be saved. The book must promise a Savior and his sacrifice, followed by his resurrection, and eternal rule, and glory. It must provide spiritual food for believers, and it must warn unbelievers. It should describe and prophesy the moving of God in world history, and explain the eternal places of heaven and hell. This and much more. Today we know it had to be all that because we have in our hands a copy of the product God designed. When we read a chapter of the Bible today, such as Hebrews 1 or Romans 12 or Revelation 21, we are reading what was in God's mind before the pens of the human authors recorded the words on parchment and papyrus.

God always wants to communicate. He knows how troubles arise when communication breaks down. So he has *spoken* loud and clear the Good News of salvation, through the living Word, Jesus (Hebrews 1:1-2), and the written Word, the Bible (Hebrews 2:1-4). The Bible is truly part of God's master plan of communication to the lost world.

If God is who the Scriptures declare him to be, we should not be surprised that he would send the Bible message to the world. Think about these things:

1. If God is *all-powerful*, he could create the universe, including the human race, after his own image.

2. If God is *love*, he would want to make the human race happy and at peace with him forever.
3. If God is *holy*, he would judge and punish any violation of that holiness.
4. If no one is without sin (Romans 3:10), then everyone is *guilty* before God.
5. If God is long-suffering and merciful, he could make a way of *forgiving* the evil of people, and he would *show* them what that way of forgiveness is.
6. If man has a conscience and spirit, he may try to avoid or appease God's judgment for his evil by such things as *good works*.
7. If there are many enemies of God in the world proclaiming *their own views* of truth and salvation, they must be false, because only God can identify once and for all what the absolute truth is.
8. If God wants to communicate to the world the *truth* about the means of salvation, we can expect him to send a message in a clear, permanent way, such as by a book. He is truly the Great Communicator.

II. Revelation

We have been thinking about the Bible's origin, which is the communicating heart of the God who is love. God wants to deliver a message to the world, and he has been doing so ever since the time of Adam and Eve.

But the word *communication* doesn't tell the whole story about God's contacts with man. We need to know more about what God is like—the one and only God (Psalm 86:10), whom no man has ever seen (John 1:18). There are countless answers to the question, What is God like? And there are other questions that need to be answered, such as, What does God do? What does he say? and, How should we respond?

Answers to questions like these are the subjects of the divine activity called *revelation.*

A. *What is God's revelation?* Revelation is God's telling us truths which we would otherwise be unable to know. The Greek word translated *revelation* (e.g., in Revelation 1:1) points to this. It comes from two Greek words meaning "cover" and "off." A literal translation of its verb form, *reveal,* is "to take off the cover." Picture a basket resting on a table, with a cover on top. We don't know what's in the basket. The owner of the basket comes along and removes the cover, and we learn what the contents are—apples! The apples were there beforehand, but it takes *revelation* (taking off the cover) to let us see them for the first time.

The Bible is God's way of taking off the cover, showing us eternal truths which we would not otherwise know. For example, we may observe that sin seems universal in the world, but our observations don't show us whether there will a final *judgment* for sin—a time when all sin will receive its just reward. But the Bible does reveal this to us: "Man is destined to die once, and after that to face judgment (Hebrews 9:27, NIV). Another example: We may observe a self-healing process in nature, such as when the bark of a tree or the flesh of our body is damaged, but we learn only from God's Bible that there can be healing of our sinful souls by the death of Jesus.

B. *Our failure in searching for truth.* The human race keeps seeking the truth. People believe they can mentally figure out what everything is all about. They use the mental gymnastics of logic and reasoning, but they fall short. They are unsuccessful because the human mind is limited. The world cannot know God through its wisdom (1 Corinthians 1:21). The most people can do is reason *about* the truth already revealed by God. They cannot reason their way *to* the truth. God is the only one who can uncover the truth for mankind. God is the only one who has spoken to the human race with that kind of finality and authority. This is revelation from "above" the world as we know it.

REVELATION FROM ABOVE

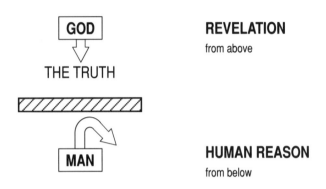

C. *Kinds of revelation.* God has chosen to reveal the truth to the world in two main ways: "general" revelation, and "special" revelation.

1. *General revelation.* This revelation comes to us from God through nature, history, and conscience. General revelation is intended to persuade lost souls to seek after God.

> **a.** *The general revelation of nature.* The supernatural works of God in creation reveal much about him. The psalmist, speaking to God, marveled that, "You have set your glory above the heavens. . . . When I consider your heavens, the work of your fingers, the moon and stars, which you have set in place, what is man that you are mindful of him?" (Psalm 8:1, 3-4, NIV). Then the apostles of Jesus declared that God ". . . has not left

himself without testimony: He has shown kindness by giving you rain from heaven and crops in their seasons" (Acts 14:17, NIV).

When Paul wrote to the Romans (1:18-23, NIV), he told them that no one—not even one who has never heard of Scripture or of a Messiah—has an excuse for not honoring God. He explained that, "what may be known about God is plain to them, because God has made it plain to them." Paul showed his readers that, "since the creation of the world, God's invisible qualities—his eternal power and divine nature—have been clearly seen, being understood from what has been made, so that men are without excuse" (Romans 1:19-20, NIV).

b. *The general revelation of history.* No nation has ever existed outside the hand of God (Romans 13:1). Again and again in Scripture we are reminded that God is always in control of all nations. "It is God who judges: He brings one down, he exalts another" (Psalm 75:7, NIV). We see God's holiness when he demands that citizens and rulers be righteous. We see his power and authority when he casts down nations. We see his mercy when he spares a land from destruction. One example of God's love and favor for a nation is his preservation of Israel down through the ages, despite wars and mass slaughters that would normally destroy a people.

c. *The general revelation of conscience.* Everyone is born with a conscience, which is an inner sense of right and wrong. Conscience points to a supreme lawgiver—that he exists, and that he distinguishes between right and wrong (Romans 2:14-15). Conscience, with its commands, warnings, and urges, makes us aware of a sin-hating God.

Those are three kinds of *general* revelation: nature, history, and conscience. Now let's focus on God's *special* way of talking to us—through the Bible and through the Savior, Jesus.

2. *Special revelation—the written and living Word.* General revelation doesn't tell the whole story of salvation. God has revealed much more than that, and we call this *special* revelation. Special revelation is God's way of making himself and the truth known specifically at special times and in special ways. Most of this revelation is recorded in the Bible. In the Old Testament it is mainly about God and his chosen people, Israel. In the New Testament the revelation is about the Son of God, Jesus Christ.

Special revelation is specific—so specific that without it we would not know the crucial truths about salvation. For example, Israelites like Abraham would not have known that salvation is by faith in God: Abraham "believed God, and it was credited to him as righteousness" (Galatians 3:6, NIV, cf. Genesis 15:6, NIV). And today we would not know that God sent his Son Jesus to the world to die for the sins of all people, so that whoever believes in him may have eternal life (John 3:16).

Most of God's special revelation has come to us through the recorded words of the Bible. This is why God sent the Bible on its journey to us. Among the Bible's main subjects are miracles, prophecies, experiences of people and nations, instruction and exhortation, and, supremely, the life and work of Christ. Let's look at those now. As we do so, we should keep in mind that these are the high points of God's message to us, the reason for the Bible's journey.

a. *Miracles.* These unusual events are signs that point to God, revealing, among other things, his presence, power, and love. John the apostle wrote in his Gospel that he reported Jesus' miraculous signs so that "you may believe that Jesus is the Christ, the Son of God, and that by believing you may have life in his name" (John 20:31, NIV). The whole Bible shows God continually at work calling sinners to follow him in faith—so it doesn't surprise us to see why he has kept on performing miracles.

b. *Prophecies.* It is often recorded in the Bible that God, usually through prophets, predicted future events that were fulfilled exactly as he had said they would be. More than a score of specific prophecies about Jesus' first coming to earth were fulfilled exactly as foretold (e.g., Jesus' birth in Bethlehem, Micah 5:2; Matthew 2:6). God's knowledge of all things and his control over the universe are clearly revealed by the Bible's prophecies. If I don't believe that God is all-powerful, I have to explain away the fulfillments of his prophecies.

c. *Experiences.* The Bible is a "people book" as well as a God book. Its main subjects are God and people. Often in the Old Testament we learn from the experiences of nations like Israel and its many enemies. Many times we read of individuals like Job who had direct communion and fellowship with God. In the New Testament we learn from people's contacts with Jesus, and we learn from the voice of the Lord in each experience—like the disciples and their Master, in the middle of a terrifying storm (Luke 8:22-25).

d. *Instruction and exhortation.* "All Scripture is . . . useful for teaching, rebuking, correcting and training in righteousness, so that the man of God may be thoroughly equipped for every good work" (2 Timothy 3:16-17, NIV). Much of the Bible is instruction in spiritual truths, and practical applications of those truths. The Bible tells us how to live and how to die. The sobering fact is that none of us can escape the accountability that comes with every instruction and command.

e. *Jesus Christ, the Son of God.* In Old Testament times God spoke to the world through his prophets. Beginning with New Testament times, he has been speaking through his Son. The final, supreme, climactic revelation given to the human race is the *person* Jesus Christ. A key Bible passage teaching this preeminence is Hebrews 1:1-3:

> In the past God spoke to our ancestors through the prophets. He spoke to them many times and in many different ways. And now in these last days God has spoken to us through his Son. God has chosen his Son to own all things. And he made the world through the Son. The Son reflects the glory of God. He is an exact copy of God's nature. He holds everything together with his powerful word. The Son made people clean from their sins. Then he sat down at the right side of God, the Great One in heaven.

Paul's letter to the Colossians is another book that devotes much space to exalting Jesus as God and Savior. In their search for truth, the people of Colossae had been depending on human wisdom for the answers. They embraced all kinds of here-

REVELATION THEN AND NOW

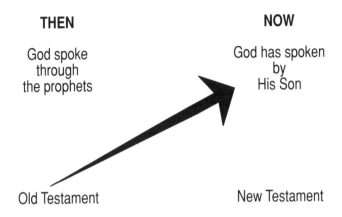

THEN

God spoke
through
the prophets

Old Testament

NOW

God has spoken
by
His Son

New Testament

sies, including the denial of Christ's deity and the worship of angels. Colossians is God's revelation to them and the world that "Christ is all, and is in all" (3:11, NIV). He is the preeminent one:

- "the image of the invisible God"
- "the firstborn over all creation"
- "by him all things were created"
- "he is before all things"
- "in him all things hold together"
- "he is the head of the body, the church"
- "all his [God's] fullness dwells in him"
- "through him [God reconciles] to himself all things"
- "[God makes] peace through his blood, shed on the cross"

(Colossians 1:15-20)

2

Inspiration— God's Revelation Is Written in a Book

What a wonderful, matchless revelation God has given to the world! He sent the Bible to us to teach truths we would otherwise not know. Think of the awesome responsibility that falls to all of us, to listen to *what God has spoken* and to respond in faith and obedience.

God has always wanted to reveal his truth to all people of the world. Before approximately 1500 B.C., there was no such book as the Old Testament. (See the chart, JOURNEY OF THE BIBLE, page 17). Before that time God chose to reveal his messages in other ways: through the preaching and teaching of prophets, through angelic messengers who spoke audible words to individuals and groups, and through his Spirit, who spoke to the hearts, spirits, and minds of the people. The Ten Commandments, given to the Israelites on Mount Sinai, are an example of spoken and written revelation given in the early years of world history, before there was a full Bible (see Exodus 20).

There was no shortage of revelation from God in those days. But there was the need of a form of special revelation that would be permanent and changeless, that would express God's message specifically and retain the full scope of revealed truth. For that, God chose the *written form* of human language recorded in a single scroll or book, to be read, learned, and applied by all. Under that plan, God wouldn't be using an endless succession of ever-changing human or angelic messengers to deliver his messages to the world. The Book would remain in the hands of the human race until the end of time, as God's full message of salvation to the world. In the words of one writer,

> If there be a God, and if He is concerned for our salvation, this is the only way (apart from direct revelation from God to each individual of each successive generation) He could reliably impart this knowledge to us. It must be through a *reliable written record* such as the Bible purports to be.[1]

We'll see in a later chapter that the Bible originally appeared in the world "piecemeal"—as sixty-six books, written by thirty-five to forty authors over a period of about 1600 years. We can get a sharper view of the making of the Bible text by visualizing a single author sitting at a desk writing one of the manuscripts with his pen. As we watch him, two questions may come to mind:

(1) How does he know what God wants him to write?
(2) How accurate is his completed manuscript?

God answers those questions in passages like 2 Timothy 3:16 (NIV) where we are told that "All Scripture is God-breathed." Another translation of that verse is, "All Scripture is given by inspiration of God" (NKJV) . In the remainder of this chapter, the phrases "inspiration of God" and "God-breathed" will appear interchangeably.

Let's look now at this important subject of *inspiration*.

I. The Fact of Inspiration

How were the books of the Bible "given by inspiration of God" (2 Timothy 3:16, NKJV)? Let's look into this.

A. *Description of inspiration.* Inspiration was God's method of having divine revelation expressed in human words. In that process, the Holy Spirit moved and guided the human authors, investing their writings with divine authority.

B. *Scripture's self-testimony.* We must accept by faith God's testimony of how the Bible came to be. If we can't believe that, how can we believe anything else the Bible says?

> If the Bible is the Word of God, as it claims to be, then it is simply impossible to appeal to any other authority . . . in order to obtain the right view of Scripture. If it is the Word of God, it is itself the highest authority; we can only submit to its claims.[2]

The Bible specifically teaches that its text was given by God, even though we may not understand the workings of that activity of God.

1. *The writings were inspired.* The key verse of 2 Timothy 3:16 (NIV) says that the Scriptures themselves were God-breathed. The metaphor of God's "breath" points to God's active involvement, implying tremendous power.

2. *The writers were inspired.* "Men spoke from God as they were carried along by the Holy Spirit" (2 Peter 1:21, NIV). The metaphor "carried along" shows how it is possible that the words written by *human* authors are *infallible*, that is, not able to be in error: this was accomplished by the sustaining work (the "carrying along") of the Spirit. The control of the Spirit over the minds of the authors was too complete and powerful to permit the human qualities of their work to contaminate the purity of the text.

3. *The authority of the text was unbreakable.* Every word written by the Bible authors had unbreakable, permanent authority, for "Scripture cannot be broken" (John 10:35, NIV).

II. The Extent of Inspiration

We have looked at the *fact* of inspiration. Now we ask how much of the Bible was so inspired. The Bible's answer is, "all Scripture." There are two words that are often used in discussions of this subject: *verbal* and *plenary*.

A. *Plenary.* Our English word *plenary* means full, or total. The Bible text says that "all Scripture" was inspired, which therefore must include words not only on spiritual and religious subjects, but on secular subjects as well—such as history, science, art, and sociology. Yes, the whole manuscript written by each author was inspired. This is plenary inspiration.

B. *Verbal.* The very *words* (verbal) of the originals were inspired. Some people believe that God only inspired the *thoughts* of the writers, not the written words themselves. But the Bible text says that the *writings* (Greek: graphe, "Scriptures") were God-breathed. This does not mean that God always or usually dictated to the author what words he must write, word for word—although sometimes the exact words of the Bible text *were* originally dictated by God, as with the Ten Commandments. Apart from such exceptions, the words the author wrote were his own words that expressed perfectly what God wanted to say. "Men spoke from God as they were carried along by the Holy Spirit" (2 Peter 1:21, NIV).

C. *Autographs.* The word *Scripture(s)* refers only to the autographs. God inspired only the *original writings*—the autographs—of the Bible authors. Any copies made from these originals at a later time were subject to error. But the autographs were infallible. This is why the word "autographs" must be included in the phrase, "verbal inspiration of the autographs."[3]

III. The Character of the Inspired Scriptures

We have said that all the very words of the autographs—the *original writings*—were inspired by God. Not just *some* of those words. Not just God's *thoughts* behind the words. We have never seen any of these original writings, but we know what their authors wrote, on the basis of ancient Bible manuscripts that still exist today. We shall see in a later chapter that the Bible we have today is virtually the same as those originals, not counting the differences of language.

A. *Inerrant and infallible.* The autographs did not contain errors, because they were infallible—*incapable* of error. They were infallible because their author, God, is infallible. God is infallible in *everything* he says or does. This infallibility applies not only to the spiritual content of the Bible, but also to such subjects as science and history written about in its pages.

1. *Scientific passages.* The Bible is not a science book, but when it makes scientific statements, they are absolutely accurate. God the omnipotent Creator would never cause or allow an inspired writer to record a faulty scientific statement about his creation. Some Bible statements may *appear* erroneous, but are not actually so. For example, the author may be using phenomenal language, the language of appearance. When Moses wrote, "as the sun was setting" (Genesis

15:12, NIV), he was describing the scene *as it appeared* to human sight. The sun appeared to be setting, though the earth's rotation was really the cause of that appearance. No one today contests the daily newspaper's use of phenomenal language when it reads, "Sunset time, 8:45 P.M."

More than that, some scientific statements of the Bible report facts not recognized by many scientists until later, such as:

> Job 26:7 (NIV)—God "suspends the earth over nothing."
>
> Isaiah 40:22 (NIV)—"He sits enthroned above the circle of the earth."
>
> Jeremiah 10:12 (NIV)—"God made the earth [mass] by his power [energy]."
>
> Colossians 1:17 (NIV)—"in him [Jesus] all things hold together." Jesus' holding force applies to everything, including the material world. The heart of every atom is composed of protons and neutrons, and the protons are repellent of each other. "Every atom of every particle of matter *should* fly apart. But the fact remains that they *don't* fly apart."[4]

2. *Historical passages.* Although a relatively few minor historical errors have crept into copies of the Bible in later centuries, the inerrant view presented here contends that the historical parts of the *autographs* were absolutely without error. Again, this is because God is infallible. He knows all things. He determines and controls all history of all times. He would not let historical inaccuracies contaminate the historical passages which he chose to include in his Book.

God knows why history must be reported accurately. Robert Mounce asks:

> The Gospel writer is either right or wrong. If he is wrong in an area where we can check him (history), how can we

rely upon his accuracy in an area where no checks are possible (doctrine)? The whole thing stands or falls together.[5]

Archaeologists have recently uncovered much to support readings of Old Testament history that earlier had been challenged as erroneous. That corroboration process continues. One famous archaeologist, formerly a doubter, writes about this:

> Thanks to modern research we now recognize [the Old Testament's] substantial historicity. The narratives of the patriarchs, of Moses and the exodus, of the conquest of Canaan, of the judges, the monarchy, the exile and restoration, have all been confirmed and illustrated to an extent that I should have thought impossible forty years ago.[6]

B. *Human-divine.* The Bible is also unique in that the divine and human activity flowed together in its original production. God began preparing the authors of the Bible books for the task of writing long before the actual day of writing arrived. Then the authors wrote (this was the human work) as they were carried along by the Holy Spirit (this was the divine work, 2 Peter 1:21, NIV). Think about this: God used the vocabulary and grammar of *human* languages to reveal such deep, far-reaching doctrines as eternal life, salvation, sanctification, and the three-part nature of God the Father, Son, and Holy Spirit!

The human personalities of the different authors of Bible books are also apparent. Nonetheless, what they wrote served only to accentuate (rather than detract from) the truth of who God is and what he does. Luke had a heart for outcasts, and when we see the repeated references to them in his Gospel we also see Jesus, the friend of man. Paul was a theologian, highly trained in the law, and when we read his long doctrinal discourses in Romans, we also see Jesus who fulfilled God's law.

God permitted each of the original human writers of the Bible text to express eternal truths in their own unique styles of writing. He knew this would add interest and impact to the text when it would be read centuries later, by people of varied backgrounds.

C. *Mystical.* The Bible is a mystical book. This is partly because it is a book of the Spirit, with a message of much mystery. It is mystical also in passages where God is withholding revelation for some reason. And the Bible's miracles have much mystery about them. The writers didn't avoid reporting the supernatural, nor did they try to explain away the miraculous. The Bible is about the movements of God, so we can expect to see miracle after miracle. We recognize and accept the miracles by faith, which does not mean we understand all the workings of the miraculous.

D. *Selective.* One of the most important characteristics of the Bible text is its selectivity. The Holy Spirit determined what should be included in the text, and what should be kept out of the writing. The original writers used their personal styles of writing, but it was the Holy Spirit who moved them as to what to include (2 Peter 1:21). He carried them along, directing their thoughts without dictating what they should write. Without this selectivity by God, the human quality of the Bible would take over.

As Bible students today, we must never add to the Bible text what God chose *not* to include, nor overlook what he *did* write.

IV. Wrong Views of Inspiration

The journey of the Bible from God to the world has not transpired without dangers and threats. One of those threats comes from people who deny how the Bible was originally inspired. There are many different interpretations of the Bible because there are different views of the

Bible's inspiration. It is important to believe correctly about how God's Book was inspired.

Having looked at the correct biblical view of inspiration, the false views should be apparent to us. Knowing what genuine money looks like is the best aid in detecting the counterfeit.

A. *Partial inspiration.* A liberal view of inspiration says the Bible *contains* the Word of God, but also contains parts which are not God-breathed. The passages that are knowable by human research or reason (e.g., history, science) need not be God-breathed. According to this view, the Holy Spirit helped the authors record only the spiritual passages, God's revelation. These were the inspired parts. This is the *partial* inspiration point of view.

Scholars in the "neo-orthodox" school of thought say that the Bible *becomes* the Word of God at the moment the reader derives a spiritual experience from a particular passage. This is a *conditional* type of partial inspiration.

The correct, plenary view is that all the very words of the autographs are God-breathed. The Bible *is* the Word of God. This is *total* inspiration.

B. *Conceptual inspiration.* This view says that the thoughts behind the words, not the words themselves, were inspired. But this leaves the door wide open to any interpretation.

C. *Dictation inspiration.* This mechanical view says that the whole Bible text originated by dictation. The authors were unconscious penmen, robots, recording what God dictated.

D. *Natural inspiration.* In this view, the Bible authors simply had natural talents (as in art and music) to write this literary masterpiece.

E. *Illumination inspiration.* This incorrect view sees the Bible text as written by individuals who claimed to have had a special spiritual experience apart from the Spirit of God. Those who accept such a false claim see the Bible as an ever-changing book, with additions and deletions made by religious leaders of cults and false religions.

It is not hard to see flaws in each of these false views of inspiration. The flaws are evident when we compare them with a more evangelical view, which states that inspiration is:

> ... the work of the Holy Spirit by which, through the instrumentality of the personality and literary talents of its human authors, He constituted the words of the Bible in all of its several parts as His written word to men and therefore of divine authority and without error in the autographs.[7]

V. Why Is Divine Inspiration of Scripture so Important?

The divine inspiration of Scripture is crucial because of what the Book reveals about God and the responses he expects. A conference of evangelical scholars has expressed it in this theological form:

> God, who is Himself Truth and speaks Truth only, has inspired Holy Scripture in order to reveal Himself to lost mankind through Jesus Christ as Creator and Lord, Redeemer and Judge. Holy Scripture is God's witness to Himself. Holy Scripture ... is to be
>
> 1.   believed, as God's instruction, in all that it affirms;
> 2.   obeyed, as God's command, in all that it requires;
> 3.   embraced, as God's pledge, in all that it promises.
>
> The doctrine of inerrancy has been integral to the church's faith throughout its history. A confession of the full authority, infallibility, and inerrancy of Scripture is vital to a sound

understanding of the whole of the Christian faith. . . . Such confession should lead to increasing conformity to the image of Christ.[8]

Yes, the authority, infallibility, and inerrancy of the Bible are crucial because a sinner's regeneration, and confession of saving faith, begin there. Divine inspiration is critical because God's message is of eternal dimensions and absolute consequences. God inspired the human writers to record the true message of salvation to man, the sinner. If that true message were reported falsely, incorrectly, or incompletely by an original author, it would violate the absolute reliability of God's voice.

We shall now look at both the Old and New Testaments to see why the messages of each Testament are vital, supreme, and indispensable, demanding divine inspiration.

A. *Key Revealed Truths Preserved by the Old Testament*

Note: As you read the next pages (41–56), observe why the key truths of the Old and New Testaments could be preserved only through the divine inspiration of infallible, inerrant Scripture.

1. *What God does always conforms to who he is.* One of the main purposes of the Old Testament is to reveal *who God is*. He is eternal Spirit, alive and personal, the first cause of all creation, himself uncaused (cf. Exodus 3:14). He is holy, righteous, just, loving, merciful, gracious, and true. He is present everywhere (Psalm 139:7-12). He knows all things (Psalm 147:5); he is powerful (Job 42:2; Jeremiah 32:17), and unchangeable (Malachi 3:6). These are some of the attributes that describe who God is all the time, absolutely and perfectly. Why would such a perfect God choose to write a faulty book to reveal who he is?

The Bible's revelation of God's nature is not dependent on our understanding of him. Example: When God sends awful judgment for sin because he is a holy God, it may appear to us that this action nullifies his grace and mercy. But God never acts contrary to his manifold nature. In our human limitations we may not always understand his workings, and we may even ask such questions as, Why does a loving God permit the indiscriminate ravages of a flood or earthquake? Even an Old Testament author may have questioned God as he wrote about such disasters, nevertheless he wrote everything *as he was inspired to write.* When we read such passages, we must see God by faith as the never-changing one, who is holy but always acts in love, and who is loving but never contradicts his holiness.

Who God is determines *what he does,* and this is perfectly revealed in the infallible, inspired Scriptures.

2. *All history is in God's sovereign control.* The Old Testament is mainly history, but it is *sacred* history. That is, it reveals especially how God moves in and through the lives of people and nations.

There are no accidents in world history. The inspired writers of the Old Testament reported that God directed or permitted the course of events in a person's career or in a nation's history according to his sovereign and perfect will. For example, God granted Israel's evil demand for kingly rule, and centuries later, in righteous judgment on those kings and their people, he sent the Babylonian conqueror. In both actions he revealed his own nature, as well as man's.

Whenever we have questions about the perplexities of Old Testament history, further study may clarify the text. In any case, we can rest confidently in the truth that God is Lord of all history, and that the inspired writers of the autographs reported events without error. For God was the source of all their information.

3. *Israel was God's divinely-called and favored nation.* How could the Old Testament writers accurately report the full story of God's calling Israel to be his favored nation? Divine inspiration was the only way. The inspired Bible text reports that God called Abraham to be the father of a nation, and then God made the nation (Genesis 12:1-2).

Just because we may be confused about why God would elect one nation to be the object of special blessing (Genesis 12:2), we should not charge the Scripture's author with inaccurate reporting. He wrote what he was inspired to write, and everything he wrote was infallible. God is *absolutely sovereign.* As we continue our Bible reading, we will learn that sovereign election applies also to God's saving of individuals (Ephesians 1:4-5). Though we cannot fully comprehend it, we may be assured that God, in the exercise of his rightful sovereignty over the entire universe, never violates his attribute of justice in the expression of his love. Such deep doctrines as these could be preserved accurately and fully in a written book only if the human author was infallibly inspired by the Spirit of God.

4. *God wanted to use Israel as his channel of communication to the rest of the world.* Israel and Israelites are the main subjects of the Old Testament from Genesis 12 to the end of Malachi. The chart, OLD TESTAMENT HISTORY (page 45), shows the eras and main events of Jewish history in the Old Testament world (which included non-Jewish nations). God moved the Old Testament writers to report this prominence of one race, even though readers would raise questions in the years to come.

God has always used people to communicate the message of salvation to other people. In New Testament times, he started with a nucleus of believers in Jerusalem, to whom Christ gave the commission, "You will be my witnesses—in Jerusalem, in all of Judea, in Samaria, and in every part of the world" (Acts 1:8). The same principle applies today—believer reaching out to unbeliever.

In Old Testament times, God wanted Israel to enjoy the fullest blessings of fellowship with him in this life, and thus be living witnesses of God's love to the nations around them. Throughout the Old Testament are recorded God's promises of salvation for all who believe, non-Jew as well as Jew. For the most part, Israel failed as God's witness during the sixteen hundred years of its Old Testament career, and that is one reason why relatively few stories of evangelistic outreach to Gentile nations appear in the Old Testament text. God did not overlook these foreign nations (e.g., Nineveh), but neither was he able to use his chosen people, Israel, to the extent that he desired.

Only the supernatural moving of the Holy Spirit upon the minds and hearts of the Old Testament writers, most of whom were Jews, would bring about the full, inerrant account of the many failures and tragedies of Israel during those centuries.

5. *Redemption is the key subject of the Old Testament.* From beginning to end, the whole Bible is the story of redemption—God's work of bringing sinners back into fellowship with him. There are other important ingredients in the story of the Old Testament, such as the Creation account and the many judgments of God upon nations and individuals. But from the time of Genesis 3, when Adam and Eve sinned and broke fellowship with God, to the last words of Malachi, the Old Testament message centers on how sinful man can be redeemed and reconciled to God.

OLD TESTAMENT HISTORY

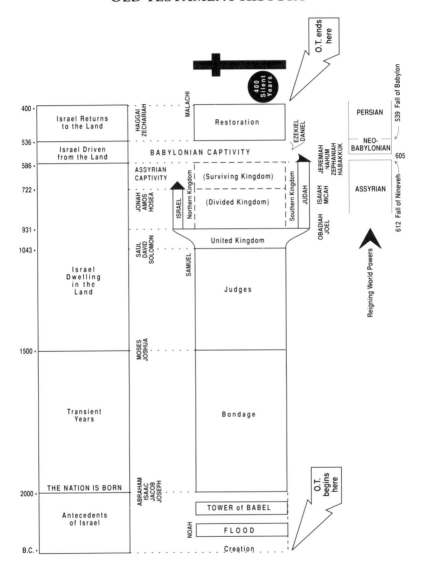

The writers used various synonyms for redemption, for example, "delivered" (Joel 2:32, KJV), "life" (Deuteronomy 30:20), "walk in the light" (Isaiah 2:5, NIV), "return" (Isaiah 55:7, KJV), and "heal" (Isaiah 57:18).

Only holy men of God, carried along by the Spirit of God (2 Peter 1:21, NIV), could write infallibly and with authority about the redemption of the soul. Here are some of the redemptive truths they recorded on their ancient scrolls:

a. God seeks to save all lost sinners, not only Israelites.

b. Spiritual deliverance is more important than physical help.

c. God may use severe measures, such as war and captivity, to bring about conviction of sin, repentance, and faith.

d. Man is saved by faith, not works. This is how Abraham was declared righteous (Genesis 15:6; Romans 4:1-3).

The writers of the Old Testament depended totally on the guidance of the Holy Spirit for what to teach about this important subject of redemption. The Holy Spirit was responsible for what each author *included* in his account, and what he *omitted*.

6. *Miracles are one of God's ways to reveal himself.* "Believe the miracle; accept the message." This statement reveals the main purpose of God in performing miracles. The Old Testament narrative is filled with miracles. Since the creation of man, a common purpose of God's miracles was to manifest his nature and to draw people's attention to what he was saying. Over and over again in pre-New Testament times, God performed miracles to turn the people's hearts to him.

Any reader of the Bible who disbelieves miracles is rejecting God by refusing to listen to God's voice. This is where most Bible critics commit intellectual and spiritual suicide. The heart of faith stands on the sure foundation that the Bible's reporting of miracles, though with the pens of human writers, was by the Spirit of God, and therefore infallible and inerrant.

7. *God has revealed the way* **to** *him and the walk* **with** *him.* Only God knew what message the human race needed to hear. And he knew that that message would remain current and contemporary throughout human history. Only divine inspiration could perform that miracle of spanning the centuries.

God's Book is timeless in its application. That's why the apostle Paul, writing to his friend Timothy about the Scriptures (which then included only the Old Testament), asserted dogmatically, by inspiration of the Holy Spirit, that "All Scripture is God-breathed and is useful for teaching, rebuking, correcting and training in righteousness, so that the man of God may be thoroughly equipped for every good work" (2 Timothy 3:16-17, NIV).

In the same context, Paul reminded Timothy that it was those sacred writings which had given Timothy the wisdom "that leads to salvation through faith in Christ Jesus" (2 Timothy 3:15). It is correct to say that all spiritual lessons derived from passages in the Old Testament have something to say, directly or indirectly, about either of those two timeless, vital life truths: *the way to God*, or *the walk with God*. The Old Testament is that contemporary.

> The words of Scripture are of God. . . . The attempt to explain them as anything less than Divine is one of the

greatest failures that has ever appeared in the history of human thought.[9]

8. *The Old Testament constantly points forward to the coming Savior and King, who is Jesus Christ.* The hundreds of Old Testament prophecies about Christ are clear evidence that the writers of those Scriptures had to be infallibly inspired. If they prophesied falsely, the credence of the whole Bible would be shattered. Divine inspiration is that crucial.

If redemption is the key subject of the Old Testament, and if Christ (the "anointed one," the Messiah) is the Redeemer of the world, then we may expect to find many Old Testament passages pointing forward to him. These may prophesy a glorious future for Israel as a nation under Christ's rule, or they may point to the blessings of salvation to each individual who believes in Christ the Savior. Isaiah 53 is a classic messianic prophecy of Christ's substitutionary death for sinners.

Many Old Testament passages foretell the person and work of Christ in the form of poetic "types" and symbols (e.g., the slain lamb), not necessarily in direct, predictive language. And throughout the Old Testament record, before Jesus appears on the earth in the flesh, he is called Son of David, Son of Abraham, the promised seed, or the heir to David's throne (Matthew 1:1; Luke 1:32; Galatians 3:16; Isaiah 9:7; Jeremiah 23:5). Jesus is the one the Old Testament saints waited for: Messiah and King (Luke 24:27, 44); priest and sacrifice (Hebrews 10:1-17); prophet and teacher (Matthew 5:17); Savior and Lord (see John 5:39).

The inerrancy of hundreds of direct and indirect prophecies about Christ, most of which have already been fulfilled, can be explained only by acknowledging that the Old Testament writers were divinely inspired.

B. *Key Revealed Truths Preserved by the New Testament*

We have been seeing in the Old Testament how its key subjects are so crucial and of eternal consequence that one hundred percent protection was mandatory in the writing stage. Only inspiration by the Spirit of God could bring about such inerrancy. Now we shall look at some of the key truths of the New Testament preserved in the same infallible inspiration.

1. *Redemption is the prominent subject of the New Testament.* The New Testament is the fulfillment of the Old Testament's story of redemption—God's work of bringing sinners into fellowship with him. God can do this through the death of his Son, Jesus, on the cross of Calvary. Jesus is the sacrifice, the Redeemer, the Savior. This is why Jesus is the prominent person of the New Testament. No wonder the cross of Calvary has been called "the central act of God" in the whole history of the universe! The accompanying chart, THE EARTHLY LIFE OF CHRIST, shows the cross as the climax of Christ's giving himself for the sins of the world.

When Jesus was crucified, many of his followers fled from the scene in unbelief, frightened and utterly confused about why their Messiah was being killed. A few days later, the report of the empty tomb confused them even more. And when Jesus appeared to some disciples after his resurrection, they did not recognize him at first. The early church did not depend solely on the first reactions of those disciples for a full, infallible record of what actually happened. Some time later, God inspired Matthew, Mark, Luke, and John to record the authoritative record for all time. Those four Gospels and the twenty-three books that follow them are God's infallible record of everything

THE EARTHLY LIFE OF CHRIST

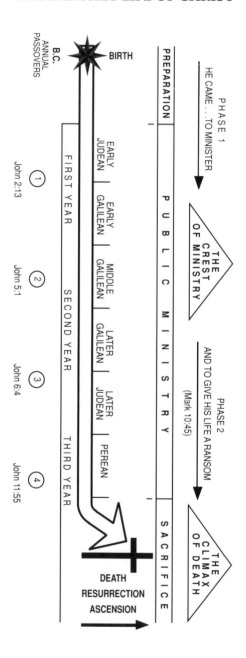

he wanted to reveal to the world in this, his new covenant (New Testament).

2. *Man's basic problem is sin.* Redemption is prominent in the New Testament because it is God's merciful response to man's basic problem, sin. The wages of sin is death (Romans 6:23, KJV), which is eternal separation from God. Just as we may expect to read much in the New Testament about salvation, it should not surprise us to see extensive coverage of sin and its judgment. Jesus spoke much about the judgment of hell. Much of Paul's letter to the Romans is about sin (e.g., Romans 1:18-3:20).

Sin estranges man from God, and that is why God judges it as the archenemy it really is. And that is also why God gave his Son to die on the cross. Christ's death is the exact measure of the sins of mankind: "he died for all" (2 Corinthians 5:15, NIV). The New Testament books record these truths perfectly. They are eternal truths, dependable only because they were infallibly inspired by God.

3. *The human race has no hope outside God's grace.* This truth is taught infallibly throughout the New Testament, even as in the Old Testament. Paul wrote that sinners, because they are separated from Christ, have no hope and are without God in the world (Ephesians 2:12, NIV). Unbelievers who refuse the gift of God's grace—who refuse to be clothed in Christ's righteousness—will spend eternity in the pain and agony of separation from him. God must send awful judgment for sin because he is a holy God. But God's grace gives a shining ray of hope. In grace, God gave the gift of his Son, who died on the cross of Calvary for the sins of mankind. Those who believe in Christ are saved by that grace. Here's what Paul wrote about God's grace:

> But God's mercy is great, and he loved us very much.
> We were spiritually dead. . . . But God gave us new life
> with Christ. You have been saved by God's grace. And
> he raised us up with Christ. . . . I mean that you have been
> saved by grace because you believe. You did not save
> yourselves. It was a gift from God. . . . In Christ Jesus,
> God made us new people . . . (Ephesians 2:4-10).

4. *The gospel of Jesus Christ is a universal message.* Jesus and his disciples preached the gospel ("Good News") first to the Jews (Romans 1:16), because they were of the favored nation descended from Abraham (Genesis 12:1-3; 17:1-8). But Israel rejected Jesus as the Messiah, and with that rejection came the extension of the call to the Gentile (non-Jewish) world. That universal audience of the gospel is what Jesus had in mind when he gave his disciples the commission, "You will be my witnesses—in Jerusalem, in all of Judea, in Samaria, and in every part of the world" (Acts 1:8). Throughout the New Testament, the gospel is shown as the power of God to save everyone who believes, Jew or non-Jew (Romans 1:16). This is the clear, infallible, authoritative message of the New Testament books, sent to the whole world.

5. *Jesus is the true God-man.* Jesus could do what he did only because of who he was, the true God-Man. He was true God and true man at the same time. We humans can't understand this supernatural fact, but we believe its truth because we have full confidence in the authoritative Book that teaches it. An example of this dual personage is Jesus as the perfect sacrifice on the cross. He was a genuine *substitute for mankind* on the cross because he was crucified as real persons were crucified. He was *true man*, genuinely human. And he was an *acceptable sacrifice* because he was sinless and perfect—true God.

The stumbling block to those who reject the *works* of Jesus (such as performing miracles) is that they do not believe him to be *who he truly is* (see Mark 8:27-31). Throughout the New Testament, the vital relationship of Jesus' *person* and his *works* is constantly brought before us. The life and ministry of Christ are an enigma if the infallible inspiration of the Bible is denied.

The divinely-inspired New Testament abounds with miracles performed by Christ. Jesus' miracles were superhuman, all-powerful acts and deeds that were evidences and proofs that he is the God and Savior he claimed to be (John 20:31). The writer of Hebrews says that Jesus' message of how to be saved is proved true by God's "using wonders, great signs, and many kinds of miracles" (Hebrews 2:3-4). Peter said on Pentecost Day, after Jesus' supernatural ascension to heaven, that "Jesus from Nazareth was a very special man. God clearly showed this to you by the miracles, wonders, and signs God did through him" (Acts 2:22).

Many of the miracles Jesus performed in the first century are recorded in the Gospel accounts. John, author of the fourth Gospel, tells the reader why he reported Jesus' miracles: "that you can believe that Jesus is the Christ, the Son of God. Then, by believing, you can have life through his name" (John 20:31).

The grand miracle of the Gospels is the bodily resurrection of Jesus from the grave (Matthew 28:1-10; Mark 16:1-7; Luke 24:1-12; John 20:1-18). The triumphant, infallible words of that event are, "He is not here—he is risen!" And the message to the world in the Book inspired by the Holy Spirit is, "Listen to what he says, and believe him to be saved!"

6. *The Holy Spirit is an active worker in this age.*
The Holy Spirit is one of the three persons of the Godhead. All three are always ministering on behalf of every creature. Their ministries are equally important, though different. The Old Testament records

ministries of the Holy Spirit to all people, but especially to the believing Jews. In the New Testament, there are many verses and extended passages which describe the Spirit's person and work in the experience of Christians.

Shortly before Jesus' arrest and crucifixion, he told his disciples that he would be leaving them for awhile, to go to his Father in heaven (John 14:1-4, 12, 28; 16:5). He and his Father would then send the Holy Spirit to them, to minister to their continuing needs (John 14:16-17, 26; 15:26). At some later time, Jesus would return to earth (John 14:18; 16:16) to join the Spirit in helping God's people (14:16).

Some key chapters describing the ministries of the Holy Spirit at this time are John 14-16 and Romans 8. From these passages we learn how important the work of the Spirit is today, especially in the daily walk of the Christian. Here are some of his ministries:

- Helper—John 14:15-17, 26; 15:26; 16:7-11; Romans 8:26
- Teacher—John 14:25; 15:26; 16:8-15
- Guide, Sanctifier, Strength—Romans 8:1-25
- Intercessor—Romans 8:26-27

A key role of the Holy Spirit was his guidance and control in the writing of Holy Scripture:

> No prophecy of Scripture came about by the prophet's own interpretation. For prophecy never had its origin in the will of man, but men spoke from God as they were carried along by the Holy Spirit" (2 Peter 1:20-21, NIV).

In 2 Timothy 3:16 (NIV), Paul identified God's part in the writing of Scripture as *God-breathing*: "All Scripture is God-breathed." So powerful was God's breathing and the Spirit's control that what was written on the original scrolls was the infallible and authoritative Word of God. With that control, an imperfect Bible autograph was impossible.

7. *All world history moves onward to the last days.* We saw earlier how Old Testament writers constantly pointed forward to the coming Savior and King, who is Jesus Christ. When the New Testament authors wrote their books, the enthronement of Christ was closer by as much as fifteen hundred years. They wrote about the earthly life of Christ (four Gospels); they reported the birth and first years of the Christian church (Acts 1-12); they described the church's early years of expansion (Acts 13-18; the epistles; Revelation 1-3); and the last writer reported visions of world history, of end times (Revelation 4-18), and of the triumph and enthronement of the King of Kings (Revelation 19-22).

Throughout the New Testament are many prophecies—detailed and general, short and long—of history yet to be. Only God can predict the future. Every prophecy penned by a Bible author was infallible because every Scripture was God-breathed, and the writers were under the control of the Spirit.

8. *The New Testament books are God's final instructions for living.* It is possible for Christians to live lives pleasing to God (see Hebrews 11:6). If that were not so, all the New Testament's commands, exhortations, promises, and helps would be one vast fraud.

The New Testament contains God's instructions on how to become a Christian and how to live the Christian life. It was written almost two thousand years ago, when it joined the corpus of inspired Scripture that had been the Bible of Jesus (Old Testament). And it remains timeless in its application. God gave it to evangelize lost sinners and to build up those who believe in his Son.

The New Testament, like the Old Testament, is the trustworthy Word of God because the autographs were inspired by the Spirit of God, infallible, inerrant, and authoritative. That is what makes the inspiration of Scripture so important.

3

Composition—
The Book Takes Shape

The book called the Bible was not the brainstorm of an eager saint, the masterpiece of a gifted author, or even the work of one solitary individual commissioned by God. No one person planned it, wrote it, published it, translated it, or distributed it to the people of the world. Then how did the Bible come about, and who was that mysterious First Cause? There is only one answer, and it is short: God did it.

Who else could span sixteen hundred years, bring together forty potential writers scattered around the world during those centuries, and with a bold, masterful stroke of all-wisdom and all-power create the Miracle Book that would never be matched?

In preceding chapters we viewed the early stages of the Bible's journey from God to us. We saw the heart of God wanting to communicate a message of love to the world. We saw him in different ways revealing the wonderful truth to mankind. We saw him inspiring authors to write unique, infallible, inspired autographs—*written* revelations of God. In this chapter we'll be looking at *composition*—seeing how the Bible took shape as the authors composed sixty-plus manuscripts which finally merged together as *one book*, which we now call the Bible.

I. One Book, the Bible

The word "Bible" is traced back to the singular Greek word *biblion*, meaning book. When all the Old and New Testament books came together, the Greek-speaking Christians called the collection *ta biblia*, "the books." Latin-speaking Christians referred to the collection as *biblia*, using the word in a singular sense, and from that Latin arose the singular English word "Bible." So from the earliest centuries, Christians recognized the unity of the Scripture of God, calling it Bible.

The largest group of Bible authors lived before Jesus' birth—they were the Old Testament writers. Some of the other authors were contemporaries of Jesus, and all wrote their scrolls by the end of the first century. They were the New Testament writers.

The forty different authors were writing their inspired autographs at different times and in different circumstances. God knew while they were writing that the finished product would turn out to be one book made up of more than sixty scrolls, a mini-library of writings by forty authors. Though there would be many books in the Book, all of them together would proclaim in some way one key message, which was salvation from sin and its judgment, by faith in Jesus Christ.

This unity of the Bible was not by accident. The New Testament writers knew what the Old Testament Scriptures said, and they quoted them from time to time. But they did not know what plans God had for a second and final group of manuscripts. Everything was under his direction.

The Holy Spirit inspired the writers to pen words in such a way that whatever they wrote supported the common theme of salvation, directly or indirectly. They wrote that God was Savior as well as Creator, as they described his person and his work. They said that saved persons were people of God, the righteous and the wise, indwelt by the Spirit. They called them the church, the saints, the believers, Christians. And they made clear what the way of salvation was: by the Lord's grace, through believing in him.

The accompanying diagram illustrates the Bible's unity of message and authorship. The large triangle represents the whole Bible and its one major message. In that outer triangle, the lower large area is the Old Testament, which is the longer part of the Bible, written by the larger number of authors. The small triangle at the top is the peak, the climax of the Bible. It is the New Testament, smaller than the Old, written by fewer authors. The Old Testament is the beginning and foundation of the Bible text, and the New Testament is the fulfillment and completion of that revelation from God.

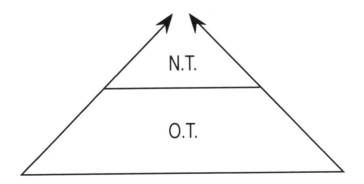

II. Two Parts, the Testaments

When we open our Bibles today to the introductory pages, one of the first things we observe is the word "Testament." On closer inspection, we notice that this large book is divided into two unequal parts: the longer Old Testament followed by the shorter New Testament. (See chart, JOURNEY OF THE BIBLE, page 17.) The Old Testament is about three times the length of the New.

On one of the Bible's opening pages there is usually a list of the books of each Testament. But that doesn't tell us how the term "Testament" is used. So it is easy for us to pass over the term, or at best to recall the familiar phrase of inheritance, "last will and testament."

Actually, the Bible word *covenant* better expresses what the Old English word *testament* is intended to mean. A study of covenants in the Bible reveals that a covenant is an agreement which God initiates by his grace with his people. In the days of Moses, the Lord made a covenant (Old Covenant) on the basis of blood sacrifices of animals, offered by the people for atonement of sins (Exodus 24:8). Later, Jeremiah prophesied that God would make a "new covenant" with his people (Jeremiah 31:31ff.). When Jesus came to this earth, he established this *new* covenant between his Father and the people, ratified by his own blood, not the blood of animals. "Christ died for us" (Romans 5:8). It was a sacrifice given "once for all" (Hebrews 10:10, NIV).

The Old Covenant failed when the people broke it by their sins. That covenant couldn't bring forgiveness once and for all, nor could it bring the power to live lives pleasing to God (Hebrews 8-10). But God in mercy continued to keep his part of the covenant, preparing the way for a superior New Covenant, which he sent his Son to inaugurate (Jeremiah 31:34).

The Holy Spirit inspired men living before the time of Christ to write about their Old Covenant days, and to prophesy a coming era, with Christ "the guarantee of a better agreement," the New Covenant (Hebrews 7:22).

Then Jesus came, and died, and was raised from the grave. After he had ascended into heaven, the Spirit moved upon the hearts and minds of nine or ten men, guiding them to write about the Christ of the New Covenant. Their narratives and letters would tell how Jesus died on the cross for the sins of the world, and was raised from the grave to assure eternal life for all who believe. Those writings would come to be known as the New Covenant, that is, the New Testament. (We use the word "Testament" rather than "Covenant" in the titles Old Testament and New Testament simply because it has become a permanent reference of identification in the English language.)

III. Many Books, Many Authors

As noted above, the opening pages of our Bibles list the names of the books of the Old and New Testaments. We count thirty-nine Old Testament books, and twenty-seven New Testament books. How did those sixty-six books, written by many authors, come together in the Miracle Book called the Bible? The answer is that God moved in the hearts of his people to *recognize* what writings of men were *not* inspired as Holy Scripture, and what writings *were* inspired. This is the story of the *canon* of the Bible, which we will be looking at in chapter 4.

IV. The Part Played by Humans in the Journey's Beginning

We have been watching the early stages of the Bible's journey, the writing of the sixty-six books. It is a Miracle Book, and it has all the qualities of a supernatural work of God. But the journey of the Bible also has some *human* parts, and it will be good for us to look briefly at some of these now.

A. *Human writers.* There were about forty writers whom the Spirit moved to compose the Bible autographs. They were as human as human can be. True, they were special for being chosen to experience the God-breathing which brought forth the Bible words they penned, but they were still human. All of them.

The last of these men lived about fifteen hundred years after the first writer. Their home areas ranged from Italy in the west to Persia in the east. Among them were a king, soldier, fisherman, herdsman, legislator, prophet, priest, physician, and rabbi. Their homes and educational backgrounds were different, as were their natural talents and gifts. For example, King David was a gifted poet, and Luke was a medical doctor. Paul was a theologian, and Mark was a news reporter. None of the authors lived a perfect life, and yet God used them to write his infallible Book. When we read the Book, we can feel the human touch while we sense the divine presence. Again we have to exclaim, "There is no book like this!"

B. *Human writings.* The writers of the Bible books were given freedom in the composing of their autographs. Their vocabularies were different, as were their subjects and styles, which included: history, poetry, law, parable, allegory, biography, autobiography, letters, testimonies, prophecy, and doctrine.

The Bible authors used the same writing materials used by other writers of their time:

1. *Papyrus.* This was paper-like material, made of the inner bark of a reed plant. Pieces were pressed and dried in flat strips and glued together. Sheets were about six to fifteen inches long and three to nine inches wide. They were joined together and rolled into a scroll. Only one side was used for writing.

Probably all the Bible autographs were written on rolls of papyrus. Under the protecting care of God, those autographs were copied before they perished, and throughout the centuries that followed, the copies have been re-copied, on and on. The perishable papyrus was eventually replaced by the more permanent material called parchment.

2. *Parchment*. This writing material was more durable and permanent than papyrus. It was made from the dried skins of animals, and was very costly. Our most substantial ancient copies of the Bible text are on parchment.

Today we have no part of an original manuscript of a Bible book, whether on parchment or papyrus. But we do have later copyings on both kinds of material.

3. *Pen and ink*. The authors wrote with pen and ink (3 John 13). The pen was a reed, pointed at the end. Ink was a mixture of charcoal, gum, and water.

4. *Roll*. When the Bible autographs were written, page-type books, called *codices* (singular: *codex*), were not yet in common use. Instead, the pieces of papyrus or parchment were glued or sewn together, making one long roll, thirty to ninety feet long. The text was written on the roll in columns of convenient width. As the roll was read, it was unwound with one hand and wound up with the other. When it was wound up, the title of the book and the author's name were written on the outside.

Following is a facsimile page of Codex Sinaiticus, one of the most ancient Greek manuscripts of the New Testament. The passage is John 21:1-25. There are no spaces between words and sentences, and no punctuation. (Occasional marks are scribal notations.) The last three circled words say, in Greek:

GOSPEL
ACCORDING TO
JOHN.

Facsimile Page of Codex Sinaiticus

5. *Divisions in the written text.* The writers of the
original Bible autographs did not use chapter or verse
divisions, which were over a thousand years away.
(Today, we can hardly imagine what it would be like
to study the Bible without any such reference points!)
Further, to conserve space, the writers left no spaces
between words or sentences. A few of them may have
used indentations to show paragraph units of
thought, like we have in our Bibles. The authors must
have been *thinking* structure as they wrote, even
though their lines did not show it. Some Old Testament passages, like Proverbs 31:10-31, are clearly
units of thought, even without indentation of lines to
show this structure.

Eventually in later editions, indentations and
markings began to appear more commonly in manuscripts to show divisions of thought. For example, the
Codex Vaticanus manuscript of the fourth century
A.D. shows Matthew 1:1-17 as a unit of four "paragraphs"; 1:1-5; 1:6-11; 1:12-16; 1:17.

It took a longer time for chapter and verse divisions to appear in editions of the Bible. Around 1227,
before the invention of the printing press, Stephen
Langton originated chapter divisions for the English
New Testament. In 1551, Robert Stephanus printed a
Greek New Testament that used verse divisions for
the first time. The first Bible (Old and New Testament) to use both chapter and verse divisions was
Stephanus's Latin edition of 1555. The first *English* Bible to use both kinds of divisions was the Geneva Bible of 1560, a predecessor of the King James Bible.

One of the great values of most modern editions
of the Bible is the format of the printed text, including
chapter and verse references. Paragraph divisions are
clearly shown, and segments (groups of paragraphs)
are made to stand out. Most study Bibles add outlines
to show the main subjects of the segments. It is a big

help to the Bible student to be aware of paragraph and segment divisions.

4

Canonization— Sixty-Six Books Come Together

We have been watching the early stages of the Bible's journey from God to us. The journey started in the heart of God, who wanted to *communicate* with all people of his creation. He had a message of salvation to give them, which they could understand only if he would reveal it to them, uncovering his truth (*revelation*). To get that message to the people, God moved and guided chosen men to write special Scriptures breathed out by him. The "breathing out" was *inspiration*, a supernatural work of God.

But the story of the journey doesn't end there. Now the question is: How did people know exactly what writings God had so inspired, since many books were being written in the world? What list (*canon*) of books could be called God's Book? That stage is *recognition* by the people of God. In his own mysterious ways, God gave his people the discernment to distinguish an inspired Scripture from a non-inspired writing. God the Spirit was the one who had inspired the writing of the Scripture text in the first place, so it was a consistent "follow-up" for him to reveal what writings had the mark of supernatural inspiration.

God was the author of *inspiration*, and he was the giver of *recognition*.

The word *canon* simply means list. For example, there are thirty-nine books in the Old Testament canon, twenty-seven books in the New Testament canon, and sixty-six books in the canon of the whole Bible. In this chapter, we will see how the Old and New Testament canons came into being. Underlying all study about biblical canon are the truths that: (1) *God determined* what books are part of the canons, and (2) *people recognized* what God has so determined.

I. Collection of the Old Testament—Thirty-nine Books

We don't know many details about how the Old Testament writings merged together into one group, called "Scriptures" by Jesus and the early Christians (e.g., Matthew 21:42). Someone has correctly said that the story of this collecting is "veiled in obscurity." God did not deem it necessary that all this historical data be preserved. The crucial thing was that the Bible text itself be preserved throughout all time. The canonical books would speak for themselves, through the ministering of the Holy Spirit. Actually, no person or group determined what books were canonical. It was God himself who canonized each portion of Scripture as it was written. Thus on the chart, JOURNEY OF THE BIBLE, page 17, we see canonization as a process that continued throughout the sixteen hundred years when the Bible was being written.

Some time after each book was written, the people of God had the opportunity to read it, discuss its merits, and apply it to their lives. From the contents of the Bible books themselves, we can tell what kinds of standards the people of God used to measure a book. God would have given them discernment to make correct evaluations over questions like these:

1. Was it written by a true man of God, such as a prophet?
2. Was there an attraction of the people to read and re-read it?
3. Did it have the ring of God's authoritative voice ("Thus saith the Lord")?
4. Did it tell the truth about God and man?
5. Did it have the power of God to transform lives?

When the people put tests like these to an inspired book, they could sense that it was different from non-inspired books—of which there were many. Little by little, the inspired writings became identified as just that: God-breathed Scriptures.

And the people were beginning to recognize *groups* of similar scrolls, just as we today assign the title of "epistles" to a group of New Testament letters. The first writings to be assigned a group title were Moses' books: "the Law of Moses" (see Deuteronomy 31:26; 1 Kings 2:3; Ezra 7:6). The common title "the Prophets" was assigned to the remainder of the Old Testament scrolls (see Matthew 5:17). But some books, like Psalms, were considered worthy of a title different from "the Prophets." Hence the addition of a third category, "the Writings."

A. *The three-group Old Testament.* There were many Jews living in the lands of Palestine and Babylonia during the centuries before Christ. Leaders among them had the responsibility for making copies of the Scriptures to preserve the sacred text for future generations. And they were among the first to break down the thirty-nine scrolls into small groups, according to similar subjects. As noted above, they saw three types: Law, Prophets, and Writings. The thirty-nine individual books are listed below according to those types:

1. *Law* **(Hebrew, *Torah*).** Genesis, Exodus, Leviticus, Numbers, Deuteronomy. These are historical books, but the title Law was assigned to them because the Law given by God through Moses was central in the Israelites' experiences of those early years.

2. *Prophets* (*Nebhi-im*). Listed in this group are the writings of prophets (called *Latter Prophets*), and also some historical books (called *Former Prophets*) whose pages illustrated and taught great prophetical principles and lessons.

> **a. *Former prophets.*** Joshua, Judges, Samuel, Kings.
>
> **b. *Latter prophets.*** Isaiah, Jeremiah, Ezekiel; and the Book of the Twelve, which is the collection of the twelve "minor prophets" of our present English Bible, from Hosea to Malachi.

3. *Writings* (*Kethubhim*). Included in this group are poetic books, historical narratives, and books read on annual Jewish holidays.

> **a. *Poetry.*** Psalms, Proverbs, Job.
>
> **b. *Narrative.*** Daniel, Ezra-Nehemiah, Chronicles.
>
> **c. *"Holiday books."*** Song of Songs, Ruth, Lamentations, Esther, Ecclesiastes. These were read especially on holy feast days of the nation.

Because of combinations of books in the above list, the total number of books is only twenty-four, which is a smaller number than the thirty-nine count of our English Bible. But actually, the Hebrew Old Testament of the above listing is exactly the text of the present thirty-nine.

DIVISIONS OF THE HEBREW BIBLE

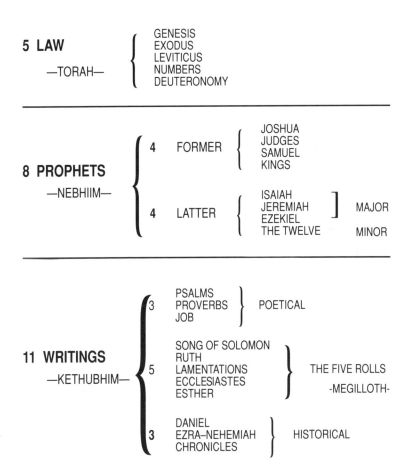

It is interesting to observe that Jesus referred to these three groups of Hebrew Scriptures just before he ascended to heaven, in full view of his disciples:

> This is what I told you while I was still with you: Everything must be fulfilled that is written about me in the Law of Moses, the Prophets and the Psalms (Luke 24:44, NIV).

In those days, the name Psalms was probably used interchangeably with the name Writings because the book of Psalms was the first and longest book of that third section.

B. *The four-group Old Testament.* Jesus often quoted from the Hebrew Scriptures. But he also freely quoted from the first foreign-language translation of the Hebrew Old Testament. This was a Greek translation, later called the Septuagint. The translation was made several hundred years before Christ, to serve the spiritual needs of Greek-speaking Jews in the Greek world, especially at Alexandria in Egypt. It is interesting to observe here that this Septuagint Bible arranged the Old Testament books in a grouping different from the Hebrew three-fold arrangement. The Greek Bible showed four groups. This arrangement was picked up by a Latin version of the Bible in the fourth century A.D., and carried over with a few changes into the list of books in our English Bible.

Many of us can recall the days of our childhood and youth when we memorized the names of the books of the Bible. We may not have been aware of the four *groups* of thirty-nine Old Testament books, because most Bibles do not print the arrangement of groups on their title pages. Here is that four-fold arrangement in the English Bible, traceable back to the Greek Old Testament:

1. *Pentateuch (five books of Moses).* Genesis, Exodus, Leviticus, Numbers, Deuteronomy. These books record the beginnings of the created universe, and the history of the chosen nation of Israel from its birth (Genesis 12) to its return to Canaan after bondage in Egypt.

2. *History.* Joshua; Judges; Ruth; 1, 2 Samuel; 1, 2 Kings; 1, 2 Chronicles; Ezra; Nehemiah; Esther. This *History* section continues the narrative of the *Pen-*

tateuch. It begins with the Jews' entrance into Canaan, and concludes with their return from Babylonian captivity.

3. Poetry. Job, Psalms, Proverbs, Ecclesiastes, Song of Solomon.

4. Prophecy. There are two groups of prophets: Major and Minor. The titles represent length more than importance (the short Lamentations is like an appendix to Jeremiah).

> **a. *Major prophets.*** Isaiah, Jeremiah, Lamentations, Ezekiel, Daniel.

> **b. *Minor prophets*.** Hosea, Joel, Amos, Obadiah, Jonah, Micah, Nahum, Habakkuk, Zephaniah, Haggai, Zechariah, Malachi.

History is prominent in the Old Testament. The Pentateuch and History books report continuous history from Adam to the Jews' return from Babylonian captivity. The next four hundred years, up to the birth of Christ, are called the "four hundred silent years" because no part of the Old Testament reports the history of those years. The book of Malachi is its last prophetic voice (written 433 B.C.).

Many chapters of the poetic books have national and biographical settings, and the books of the prophets focus on the spiritual life of the Jews and their international confrontations with neighboring enemies.

Why so much history in the Old Testament? God could have inspired the Bible authors to write only about doctrines and theological descriptions of God, sinful man, and salvation. Instead, the Spirit moved them to report life in action, doctrine put to the test, and character portraits in everyday behavior. When we read about God in the Old Testament, we watch him listening to the cries of a bereaved mother; speaking judgment through the voices of his fiery prophets; showing mercy to sinners over and over again. That's how the Old Testament reveals God to us, and prepares us for the coming of his Son. The Son is the Old Testament's promised Messiah, whom God sends to earth to walk the streets, to talk with souls, to love all enemies, and finally to give himself over to die for their sins.

II. Books Not Accepted Into the Old Testament Canon

While God was inspiring men to write what would ultimately be recognized as part of the thirty-nine-book canon, many other scrolls were being written that would remain outside the canon. The two main kinds of these are pseudepigrapha and apocrypha.

A. *Rejected by all: Pseudepigrapha.* The name pseudepigrapha means false authorship. The books falsely claim to be written by Bible authors. They were written between 200 B.C. and A.D. 200. Most of them are about dreams, legends, magic, and visions of a future kingdom. They were not regarded as canonical by Jesus, by the Jews, by New Testament writers, and by leaders of the early church. One example of each group is cited here:

1. **Legend:** Book of Adam and Eve
2. **Apocalypse:** Book of the Secrets of Enoch
3. **Doctrine:** 3 Maccabees
4. **Poetry:** Psalms of Solomon
5. **History:** Fragment of a Zadokite Work

B. *Accepted by some: Apocrypha.* The term *apocrypha* means hidden. There are various views as to why this name was assigned to these writings. The books were written between 300 B.C. and A.D. 100. Today, when we use the group name Apocrypha alone, we are referring to that time period (other "apocryphal" books were written in New Testament times and later).

Some subjects of the "hidden" books are much like those of the pseudepigraphal books. The variety is seen in the following list of the Apocrypha:

1. **History:** 1 Esdras, 1 and 2 Maccabees

2. **Religious fiction:** Tobit, Judith, additions to the canonical Esther, additions to the canonical Daniel

3. **Ethics and wisdom:** Ecclesiasticus, Wisdom, Baruch, Prayer of Manasseh

4. **Apocalypse:** 2 Esdras

In 1546, the Roman Catholic Council of Trent declared full canonical status to all the above-named Apocrypha except 1, 2 Esdras and Prayer of Manasseh. This was confirmed by the Vatican Council of 1870. Luther's German Bible of 1534 was the first printed Bible to separate the apocryphal books from the thirty-nine canonical group. This started a growing trend of omitting the apocryphal books from Protestant Bibles, or, at most, including them in the closing pages with a separate introduction showing them to be non-canonical. Today, Roman Catholic Bibles print the apocryphal books in the sequence of the thirty-nine, regarding them as having a deuter-canonical status (that is, of secondary importance). Most Protestant Bibles omit the Apocrypha completely.

The question is often asked why the apocryphal books are not accorded the same authority as the canonical books. F. F. Bruce says,

> The answer is . . . that they were not regarded as canonical by the Jews, either of Palestine or of Alexandria; and that our Lord and his apostles accepted the Jewish canon and confirmed its authority by the use they made of it, whereas there

is no evidence to show that they regarded the apocryphal literature (or as much of it as had appeared in their time) as similarly authoritative.[10]

III. Collection of the New Testament— Twenty-seven Books

The last words God ever wrote to man are recorded on the pages of the New Testament. When we read the Old Testament, we learn about God's ways especially with one people, his chosen nation Israel, and their appointed task in the world. The New Testament enlarges the scene, for here we see God's ways with the whole world, and its salvation through the gospel preached everywhere. The Old Testament prophesies Jesus' advent, and the New Testament reports it as fulfilled history. The New Testament is the outcome of the Old Testament's origins, heir of its promises, fruit of its seed, peak of its mountain.

A. *Fifty years in writing.* There was already a "Bible" when the first New Testament books were being written. Usually that Bible was referred to as the "Scripture(s)" (Matthew 21:42). As noted earlier, we now call it the Old Testament. It was the complete Bible of Jesus and the apostles. Then, a couple decades after Christ's ascension to heaven, the Holy Spirit began to move and inspire chosen saints to write more Scriptures. These autographs were letters and historical accounts that would eventually be brought together in a volume to be known as the New Testament. Its message would include the fulfillment of the prophecies of the Old Testament. The writers were not aware that what they were writing would some day be combined with other contemporary autographs to comprise this New Testament.

The New Testament books were about fifty years in writing. In our natural curiosity, we look for answers to some questions about this. For example, what was the first New Testament book to be written, and what was the last? What was the first Gospel to be written? We don't have precise answers to most questions about time lines, because dates are not part of the Bible text. But many dates of writing have been accurately determined, usually by associating the author with historical references in various New Testament books. The accompanying chart, A CHRONOLOGICAL ORDER OF THE WRITING OF THE NEW TESTAMENT BOOKS[11] shows that the epistle of James may have been the first New Testament book written (A.D. 45), and Revelation may have been the last autograph (A.D. 96). Two other interesting observations we make on this chart are that the Gospels were not the first books written, and that no book was written in the decade of 70-79. That was the decade following the destruction of Jerusalem in A.D. 70.

B. *The order of books in our New Testament.* We take for granted that soon after the last New Testament book was written, the twenty-seven books fell into place by popular agreement as one unit and in the order in which we now have them. Actually, it took a few hundred years before the canon of the twenty-seven—not more books, and not fewer—became firm and final in the view of virtually all of Christendom.

Look at the accompanying chart, CANONICAL ORDER OF NEW TESTAMENT BOOKS, and note the order of the twenty-seven numbered books. This is the New Testament canon, recognized by the people of God as the God-breathed Scriptures joining the canon of Old Testament books.

Next we will be seeing how this twenty-seven-book canon came to be.

C. *How the twenty-seven New Testament books came together.* We saw earlier that the details of how the thirty-nine Old Testament books merged into one canon

A CHRONOLOGICAL ORDER OF THE WRITING OF THE NEW TESTAMENT BOOKS

(WRITINGS OF PAUL LISTED CHRONOLOGICALLY WITH THE OTHER NEW TESTAMENT BOOKS)

BIOGRAPHY OF PAUL	BOOK	AUTHOR	PLACE WRITTEN	DATE A.D.	Personnel	Apostolic Literature	Church
	JAMES	JAMES	Jerusalem	45			
FIRST MISSIONARY JOURNEY							
—Interim—	GALATIANS		Antioch	48			
SECOND MISSIONARY JOURNEY	1 THESSALONIANS	PAUL	Corinth	52	FIRST PAULINE PERIOD	BEGINNINGS —about 15 years	FOUNDING
	2 THESSALONIANS		Corinth	52			
THIRD MISSIONARY JOURNEY	1 CORINTHIANS		Ephesus	55			
	2 CORINTHIANS		Macedonia				
	ROMANS		Corinth	56			
ARREST; FROM JERUSALEM TO ROME	MATTHEW	MATTHEW	Jerusalem?		FIRST HISTORICAL RECORDS		
	LUKE						
	ACTS	LUKE	Rome	61			
FIRST IMPRISONMENT	COLOSSIANS	PAUL	Rome	61	CENTRAL PAULINE PERIOD	CENTRAL —about 10 years	ESTABLISHING
	EPHESIANS						
	PHILEMON						
	PHILIPPIANS						
RELEASE	1 TIMOTHY	PAUL	Rome	62	PAUL'S LEGACY		
	TITUS						
SECOND IMPRISONMENT; THEN DEATH	2 TIMOTHY			67			
	HEBREWS	?					
	JUDE	JUDE					
	1 PETER	PETER		68	PETER'S LEGACY		
	2 PETER						
	MARK	MARK		?			
FALL OF JERUSALEM				70		15 "silent" years	
	JOHN	JOHN	Ephesus	85	JOHN'S LEGACY	CLOSING —about 10 years	CONTINUING
	1 JOHN						
	2 JOHN						
	3 JOHN						
	REVELATION		Patmos	96			

CANONICAL ORDER OF
NEW TESTAMENT BOOKS

HISTORY	1. MATTHEW 2. MARK 3. LUKE 4. JOHN 5. ACTS	

EPISTLES	6. ROMANS
	7. 1 CORINTHIANS
	8. 2 CORINTHIANS
	9. GALATIANS
	    10. EPHESIANS
	    11. PHILIPPIANS
	    12. COLOSSIANS
	        13. 1 THESSALONIANS
	        14. 2 THESSALONIANS } to churches
	
	           15. 1 TIMOTHY
	           16. 2 TIMOTHY
	           17. TITUS } to individuals
	           18. PHILEMON
		PAULINE

	19. HEBREWS
	20. JAMES
	    21. 1 PETER
	    22. 2 PETER
	    23. 1 JOHN
	    24. 2 JOHN
	    25. 3 JOHN
	    26. JUDE
		NON- PAULINE

VISIONS	27. REVELATION	

are mainly unknown to us. But by the time of Jesus, that Old Testament canon was a firm fact of history. For the New Testament canonization process, we have a number of specific facts. Before we look at some of these, it will help to have clearly in mind the part played by God and by the Christian communities concerning the canonization:

1. God inspired the writing of the books that would become part of the New Testament canon. Through the Holy Spirit he gave his people light to recognize which books he had inspired.

2. Public recognition of a book was not by decree of any one person, or small group, or church council. It was the collective persuasion of the communities of believers, over a period of time, to recognize which books God had inspired as Scripture.

3. In a real sense, the New Testament canon originated when the Scriptures were written. (See how this is shown on the chart, JOURNEY OF THE BIBLE, page 17.)

4. The Holy Spirit had an active part in steering the canonization process. This culminated in the list of twenty-seven books—no more and no fewer. This was important because there were hosts of religious books being written during the first couple centuries which were *not* inspired by God. Some of these were the Gospel of Thomas, Acts of Paul, Apocryphal Epistles (letters supposedly between Christ and the king of Edessa), and the Apocalypse of Peter.

All the New Testament books had been written by the end of the first century. (See chart, CHRONOLOGICAL ORDER, page 78.) The four Gospels, written at different times, eventually merged into a group called *The Gospel*.

Each Gospel kept its identity with titles like *The Gospel According to Mark*. Paul's inspired letters came together under the title, *The Apostle*, with individual titles like *The Apostle to the Romans*. The book of Acts attached itself to *The Gospel*, being the continuation of *The Gospel According to Luke*; and it also related to *The Apostle*, since Acts is the historical setting of Paul's letters. Scrolls by a few other authors were catching the people's attention during those early years, especially if the writers were apostles of the Lord.

As of the end of the first century, all the original twenty-seven scrolls of the yet-to-be New Testament had been written, but they were scattered throughout the Christian world. Neither the authors of the scrolls, nor the people of God, were aware that those twenty-seven books would someday come together as a New Testament, the counterpart of the Old Testament. Nor did they know that the final merger would not yet happen for several hundred years!

Some of the events of A.D. 100-400, leading up to the New Testament merger, are listed here:

1. *Canon of Marcion—A.D. 140.* This radical list helped wake up the Christian church. Marcion was a heretical teacher of Asia Minor. His complete canon was a reckless, abridged version:

a. *The Gospel*—only a shortened Luke.

b. *The Apostle*—ten edited Pauline epistles, minus the letters to Timothy and Titus. All Old Testament references were omitted from the letters.

2. *Two good things happened over Marcion's slashed canon:*

a. *The church began to see the need to define the canon*: four Gospels, not one; thirteen (or fourteen) Pauline epistles, not ten; plus the book of Acts and writings of other apostles besides Paul.

b. *Muratorian Canon—A.D. 170.* This list, though deficient, was an "orthodox counterblast" to Marcion. All books are named except Hebrews, James, and 1, 2 Peter.

3. *Delayed acceptance of some books.* During those early years seven of the inspired books were questioned by some believers as to whether they should be granted the same status as the others. For example, some thought James overstated the importance of works in the Christian life. Other "antilegomena" books were Hebrews, 2 Peter, 2, 3 John, Jude, and Revelation.

4. *Almost all non-canonical books dropped.* By the end of the third century, practically all non-canonical books were dropped off the growing list of "the twenty-seven."

5. *Edict of Diocletian (A.D. 303).* This anti-Christian emperor decreed that all church buildings be razed to the ground and all Scriptures be destroyed by fire. This did much to motivate the Christians to settle the question over which books were part of the inspired Scriptures. A positive motivation came about twenty-five years later when the Christian emperor Constantine encouraged and sponsored the copying and preserving of Bibles.

6. *Athanasius—A.D. 367.* This bishop's list is the first known list of the twenty-seven books.

7. *Jerome (340-420), Augustine (354-430), Council of Hippo (393), Third Council of Carthage (397).* All these recognized the twenty-seven books as the New Testament canon. From then on, the twenty-seven-book canon would be the recorded witness of the Christian church. "The Church assuredly did not make the New Testament; the two grew up together."[12]

D. *The three-group New Testament.* Look back at the chart, CANONICAL ORDER OF N.T. BOOKS (page 79), which shows the list of twenty-seven books as they appear in our New Testament. The following chart, THREE-GROUP NEW TESTAMENT, shows the three kinds of books in that list: history, epistles (letters), and visions.

> **1.** *History.* The four Gospels and Acts record the historical facts of Jesus' life, his church, and Christianity.

> **2.** *Epistles.* The epistles teach all the basic Christian doctrines, and apply them to everyday life. Paul wrote thirteen letters (or fourteen if he wrote Hebrews). The journey letters are to churches which Paul visited on missionary journeys. He wrote the prison epistles from jail in Rome. In his pastoral letters, he counseled two close friends how to shepherd their church congregations.
> The general epistles were written by other authors. They are called "general" partly because they were addressed to Christians in general, not to specific local churches.

> **3.** *Visions.* The book of Revelation is the climax of God's Book, foretelling the last chapter of world history. By many visions and symbols, it prophesies God's final judgments for sin and the eternal new heaven and new earth prepared for the followers of Jesus Christ.

THE THREE-GROUP NEW TESTAMENT

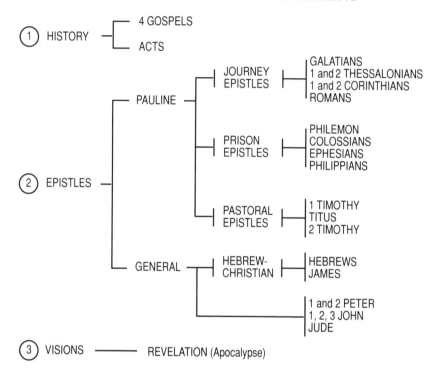

5

Transmission—
The Sixty-Six Books
Are Copied and
Distributed

What a world-shaking phenomenon we are finding this to be—the Bible's journey from God to the world! The journey had originated with God's heart-desire to communicate with the people he created by revealing the truth to them. He inspired a variety of authors to write this revelation on scrolls, and later the Holy Spirit enlightened believers to recognize which messages he had so inspired. The first thirty-nine inspired messages emerged as the Old Testament canon, and the remaining twenty-seven became the New Testament canon. Then both merged into one book.

Those sixty-six scrolls were unique, to be sure. They were the original autographs of the Miracle Book that would some day be the world's most circulated book! But sixty-six scrolls by themselves couldn't minister to billions of souls yet to be born. For one thing, the scrolls would be vulnerable to destruction by fire, water, termites, rot, mishandling, or even deliberate efforts by God's enemies to destroy it. Yet God chose to go this natural, earthbound route—under his hidden control. Owners of the autographs would have copies made before any of them perished. The sequence after that would be *copies of the copies*—and millions of copies down through the centuries. It was a *natural* route, but the *supernatural* was involved. God would supernaturally protect the copiers and their copies from ever causing crucial, spiritual harm to a reader by any human error.

The word assigned to this activity of copying is "transmission." The ultimate purpose of transmission was, and still is, getting a copy of the Bible into the hands of everyone.

I. The Transmission Process

The authors of the Bible autographs must have had some awareness of the presence of the Holy Spirit as he moved their hearts and minds to write the infallible text. And what about the hosts of transcribers as they sat at their desks and made copies of the sacred Scriptures? They didn't have the same spiritual experience as the writers of the original God-breathed Scriptures, but surely they cherished the wonderful privilege of sharing the Word of God with family, neighbors, religious leaders, and the next generation of believers. They had a part, and Isaiah included them when he wrote, "How beautiful is the person who comes over the mountains to bring good news" (Isaiah 52:7, International Children's Bible, New Century Version).

There are many stories of the multiplication of copies of the Bible. About twenty years after the Roman Emperor Diocletian's 303 decree to destroy all Scriptures, Diocletian's successor, Emperor Constantine, had the deep satisfaction of undoing some of that damage. Among other things, he ordered that fifty copies of the Bible be made and deposited in fifty churches for reading by all the people. In his own words, the copies were to be "written on prepared parchment in a legible manner, and in a convenient, portable form, by professional transcribers thoroughly practiced in their art."[13]

More than a thousand years later, with Gutenberg's invention of movable type for the printing press, the era of printed Bibles began. This has multiplied the potential ministry and outreach of the church to a degree practically unlimited.

Sometimes there was the ultimate price to pay for the spread of the Bible, like the martyrdom of translator William Tyndale (1536). In his dying moment, being burned at the stake, he cried with a loud voice, "Lord, open the King of England's eyes." The answer came three years later, when King Henry VIII placed a copy of the Bible in every church in England, with the injunction, "In God's name, let it go abroad among our people!"

Christians today rejoice over reading annual reports about the distribution of Bibles to every nation. One such report attaches this word of encouragement to all who support the work: "Your ministry is part of the global effort to share the most important information the world has ever known—the Good News of Jesus Christ."

A. *Transcribing.* Copying from another copy was a slow process, partly because the transcriber worked to avoid even one small scribal slip, such as a misplaced letter. He wrote on leather parchment or paper-like papyrus. Sometimes copies were made in group projects: one reader read from his copy while several transcribers wrote what the reader dictated. This was an efficient way to make multiple copies.

B. *Printing.* Johannes Gutenberg invented movable type for a printing press, and the first substantial work to come off a printing press was the Gutenberg Bible of 1456. This was a Latin version of two volumes, containing thirteen hundred pages of type. The task of typesetting took six years.

Before the early fifteenth century, single copies of the Bible were laboriously done by hand. Since then, the printing presses have sent out editions of thousands of copies at a time. It is not hard to see why the printing press fills such an important place in the Bible's journey.

II. How Accurate Is Our Old Testament?

We have already seen that the occasional committing of errors is part of the transmission process. But the accuracy of transmission of the Hebrew Old Testament over the centuries has been phenomenal. Dating back to Ezra's time (ca. 450 B.C.), there were special guilds of scribes whose vocation was to preserve and hand down an error-free Bible text to the next generation. The scribes had such a veneration for the written Word of God that they regarded even a single minor error of copying as a sin. If an error was made, the whole manuscript was destroyed. In later centuries, Jewish scholars called Masoretes carefully examined all existing copies of the Old Testament, looking for any kind of error. They withdrew imperfect copies from circulation as a safeguard against spreading the contamination. From this searching and comparing of manuscripts, the Masoretes were able to preserve the continuity of a virtually pure Old Testament text.

To insure exact transmission of the Bible text, the Masoretes developed a system of markings and notes which they wrote in the margins of the manuscripts, to be used as checks by the next copier. They would note such things as:

- the number of times each letter of the alphabet occurred in each book
- the middle letter of the scroll's Pentateuch and the middle letter of the whole Hebrew Bible

- the middle letter of each page
- a count of letters and words in each column.

With such dedication and high standards on the part of scribes, it isn't hard to see why the Hebrew Old Testament has been preserved so well through the centuries.

A. *We have some ancient Hebrew Old Testament copies.* For various reasons, only a relatively few Hebrew copies of Scripture survived the centuries after Christ. One reason, noted above, is that copies were destroyed if any errors were found in them. Most of the Old Testament text of our English Bible today is based on Hebrew manuscripts written after A.D. 890, in addition to manuscripts of other languages. All these Bibles supply abundant evidence of what the original Hebrew Scriptures looked like. Some of the main Hebrew manuscripts dated after 890 are listed here (the word *codex* signifies the manuscript was in *page* form, rather than a *scroll*):

1. Cairo Codex (A.D. 895). Oldest known Masoretic manuscript of the prophetic books.

2. Leningrad Codex of the Prophets (A.D. 916).

3. Aleppo Codex (A.D. 930) of the whole Bible. The most valuable Hebrew manuscript.

4. Leningrad Codex. (A.D. 1008). Largest complete Hebrew manuscript of the Old Testament.

Then in 1947, in God's design, came "the greatest manuscript discovery of modern times"—the discovery of the Dead Sea Scrolls. We will talk about this later. Virtually all aspects of that discovery support the accuracy of the codex copies listed above.

B. *Confirmation by Greek copies.* The common language of Alexandria, Egypt, during the third century B.C.

was Greek. Greek-speaking Jews living there at that time wanted their Hebrew Scriptures translated into their mother tongue, and this brought about the Greek version called the Septuagint. All of the Old Testament was translated into Greek by 180 B.C.

In the mid-nineteenth century two Greek manuscripts of the whole Bible were discovered—Codex Sinaiticus and Codex Vaticanus. The Old Testament of these manuscripts is the Septuagint version. These copies had been made by scribes in the fourth century A.D. Of all Greek copies of the Old Testament, these two have given the most help to Bible editors in reconstructing, by way of translation, what the original Hebrew Bible looked like.

C. *Other non-Hebrew witnesses of the Old Testament.* In the early centuries after Christ, a number of non-Hebrew versions appeared, translating the text of the Old Testament. Ancient copies of these, discovered by archaeologists, are witnesses to the text of the Hebrew Old Testament. Among these translations are the Syriac, Coptic, Ethiopic, and Armenian versions.

D. *Confirmation by the Dead Sea Scrolls.* In the years 150 B.C. to A.D. 70 a monastic community of Jews lived in the Judean hills near Qumran, northwest of the Dead Sea. The Hebrew Old Testament was one of the books by which they lived. In A.D. 70, when they realized that the Roman armies were invading Palestine, they hid their Hebrew scrolls in nearby caves. About two thousand years later (1947), a young shepherd boy discovered ancient scrolls in jars in a cave of the area. In the years that followed, other scrolls were found in many nearby caves—some five hundred books in all. About one hundred of these scrolls record parts of the Old Testament in Hebrew—all of Isaiah, plus parts of every other Old Testament book except Esther. Later, professional scientific examinations of the scrolls dated the writing to be about 150 B.C. When the Isaiah scroll text was compared with that of the Masoretic manuscripts of a thousand years later (listed above), the readings of both manuscripts were virtually the same! This was true also when the fragments of each Old Testament book were compared with those parts of the Masoretic text. So the Dead Sea Scrolls are powerful witnesses that the Old Testament of our English Bible today, aside from the language differences, is the same as the Old Testament of 150 B.C., and the same as the Hebrew Scriptures which Jesus used!

III. How Close to the Originals Is Our New Testament?

No book, secular or religious, comes to us from the ancient world with more *abundant* evidence of faithfulness to the original autographs than does the New Testament. We have seen that the integrity of our Old Testament is supported by the intensive care of the scribes in copying. The closeness of our New Testament to the originals is verified by the *multiplicity* of excellent copies that have come down to us. We have more than five thousand ancient Greek copies of all or part of the New Testament!

We've already seen that there were no errors in the original *autographs* of Scripture, because of the infallible inspiration by the Holy Spirit. But God has allowed some errors (very few) in the written or printed *copies* of the Bible—just as any Christian leader today may commit an error in quoting a Bible verse by memory. Most of the errors in New Testament copies were of the kind that can be detected quickly, such as the omission of a word, or repetition of a line.

In 1653, one English Bible edition omitted the word "not" from 1 Corinthians 6:9, thus giving us: "The unrighteous shall inherit the kingdom of God." The same word was omitted from Exodus 20:14 in a 1631 Bible, resulting in: "Thou shalt commit adultery." This edition was called "The Wicked Bible," and the printer was fined

ORIGINALS	COPIES
A.D. 100	
✝ VERBAL **PLENARY** (100%) INSPIRATION	NECESSARY PRESERVATION (**PARTIAL**—99%)

and all copies destroyed. But unintentional, typographical errors like these are explainable because of the human element in the transmission process.

Such errors are easily corrected because the *whole* Bible is the measuring standard for the corrections. More difficult to resolve are such questions as, "Was the passage John 7:53-8:11 in the original autographs?" The King James translators say yes, because the *largest number* of ancient manuscripts included it. But some modern translators have said no, because the *oldest* manuscripts have omitted it. Such a problem may never be resolved, unless new light from God will prove to the world whether the oldest or the largest number of witnesses are correct, in those few passages. Aside from that kind of difference, Bible editors have been able to virtually reconstruct what the original New Testament readings were. And these scholars have concluded emphatically that *no doctrine of Scripture is broken by any such manuscript variation.* Philip Schaff writes that "not one difference of reading affects an article of faith or a precept of duty which is not abundantly sustained by other . . . undoubted passages."[14]

We can have complete confidence in the text of the Bible that has been handed down to us, for the protective hand of God is the key to its preservation in transmission.

G. Douglas Young wrote the following modern parable to illustrate the power of the multitude of ancient Bible manuscripts:

> Let us consider the yardstick. For years I had an old one in my home which usually stood on its end in a corner of the kitchen. As this was moved from place to place, knocked about, packed and unpacked, the corners of it got rounded. Once it was used too drastically and the end split. Later on, after it split, a part of the end which had been split was broken off and lost. However, it was still a yardstick and it could measure 36 inches.
>
> Now let us suppose that you would come to my house to buy some goods and that I would bring out this yardstick to measure the goods. Although it was still 36 inches, because it was rounded on the edges and a part of one end was gone, it would not be surprising to me if you would raise your eyebrows at using this stick for the basis of charging you. We could suppose that my feelings would be hurt and I would say, "All right, if you won't use my yardstick, let's go to the state capital and get from the Bureau of Weights and Measures the state standard and we'll measure by that."
>
> Perhaps by this time you would want to make it difficult for me, and say, "Nothing doing. We'll go to the Bureau of Weights and Measures at the national capital. There we'll get *the* standard yardstick."
>
> Well, the fact of the matter is that we do have standard yardsticks in the state capitals and we do have a standard yardstick at Washington. Supposing that an atomic bomb destroyed the state capitals and the national capital. Would this mean that we would never again be able to measure with yardsticks? You answer, of course, that that is absolutely ridiculous.
>
> How would we then restore the standard yard? A very natural way would be to call in all of the existing yardsticks from across the country. Every man would bring in his wooden yardstick. Every woman would bring in her tape measure. What would we do with these tape measures and yardsticks? We would lay them out on a table, putting one end of each yardstick flat against a wall and then we would strike an average of the other ends. It would be no problem whatsoever to restore from the inferior tape measures and yardsticks of the nation the average, which would be the new standard yard. Just to think about the illustration is to make

one realize how ridiculous it is. The amount of variation over the 36-inch span of the yardsticks of our nation would be really infinitesimally small. Some would be a whisker short, and some would be a whisker long. The average would be easy to strike.

In our illustration the original manuscripts of the Bible are like the standard yardstick at Washington. The early copies of the manuscripts, all of them also lost, would be like the ones in the state capitals. The existing manuscripts would be like the normal yardsticks we have in our homes and and shops all across the country. Some of these manuscripts are in the language in which the original was written. Some of them are translations (versions) into other languages of the world. But when we call them all in and strike an average between all the variations, it is no more difficult to restore the original than it would be to restore the original yardstick.[15]

Back to the original question: "How close to the original autographs is our present New Testament?" Answers from many New Testament scholars are like Frederic G. Kenyon's, who writes:

> The number of manuscripts of the New Testament, of early translations from it, and of quotations from it in the oldest writers of the Church, is so large that it is practically certain that the true reading of every doubtful passage is preserved in some one or other of these ancient authorities. This can be said of no other ancient book in the world.[16]

Following are some of the main kinds of writings Kenyon cites as bearing witness to the authenticity of the New Testament:

A. Greek manuscripts. The greatest New Testament discoveries by archaeologists have been ancient Greek manuscripts. There are more than five thousand of these. The manuscripts are of two kinds: papyrus fragments (A.D. 100-300), and primary uncials (A.D. 300 ff.). The most important are the uncials.

1. Papyrus fragments. We have more than seventy-five papyri. The Rylands Papyrus, recording only five verses of John 18, is the oldest New Testament manuscript existing today (ca. A.D. 117-138). It was written by a scribe some thirty years after John had written the original text! The Chester Beatty Papyri are the most important, recording most of the New Testament. They have been dated around A.D. 250.

2. *Primary uncials.* These are the most complete Greek manuscripts of the New Testament. Some of them also record the Greek Old Testament (Septuagint version). The writing was on codex pages of durable parchment (animal skin), as compared with the paper-like papyri. The uncial printing was of large, capital letters (this type of writing gave way to small, cursive style by the tenth century).

The two oldest major uncials were written in the fourth century. The Sinaiticus Codex (A.D. 340) is the most famous and most complete copy of the New Testament. The Vaticanus Codex (A.D. 325-350) may be the oldest uncial. There are other valuable uncials, dated in the fifth century and later.

All the New Testament text is recorded in the sum of the ancient Greek manuscripts.

B. *Bible versions of other languages.* In addition to bearing the Good News of God's salvation to their readers, ancient copies of Bibles in non-Greek languages have contributed to the process of identifying what the original lines of the Greek New Testament autographs must have been. For example, when Jerome translated the New Testament into Latin (A.D. 383), his primary source was the Greek New Testament. So by translating Jerome's Latin version, New Testament scholars have learned much about how the Greek New Testament read in Jerome's time (fourth century).

In the next chapter we will be looking more at translations of the Bible, and at that time we will see listed the various versions that appeared in the early centuries.

C. *Quotations by early Christians.* We have thousands of ancient manuscripts from the first few centuries written by early church fathers, in which they quote verses of Scripture. Often the writer was a church worker or theologian, writing on official papers. A typical informal quote by an early Christian would be the quoting of John 3:16 in a letter to an unbeliever. For various reasons, such quotations from the New Testament are not as reliable as other witnesses. But they do add to the total picture, because so many of them have been discovered— more than thirty-six thousand! Almost the entire New Testament could be reconstructed from existing quotes made in the first three centuries.

D. *Lectionaries.* Lectionaries were the public church service manuals, which usually contained printed sections of the New Testament. About two thousand lectionaries have been discovered.

IV. Preservation

What does all of this chapter on transmission add up to? Preservation. Of all books written in the world, none comes near to the preservation record of the Bible. Because this Bible is a Miracle Book, its preservation will remain to the end of time. (Note how this is shown on the chart, JOURNEY OF THE BIBLE, page 17.)

When a new English New Testament is published today, the basic Greek text used by its editors has been mainly the United Bible Societies' *Greek New Testament* (1966). The reading of this standard Greek text reflects all the sound witnesses cited above, ancient and modern, that were part of the Bible's history up to that point.

6

Translation— The Bible Is Read and Studied in the Languages of the World

The translation of the Bible into languages of the world is the crucial final stage of the Bible's miracle journey. We have seen that the original autographs were written in Hebrew, Aramaic, and Greek, languages that later would be foreign to most people of the world. If God were to communicate to all people groups of the world by way of a written message, we can see why it would have to be in the mother tongues of those people. Only then could they read, and study, and understand. And that is what happened. And it is still going on, by translators from such groups as Wycliffe Bible Translators. The American Bible Society reports that, as of the end of 1988, there were 1,907 languages of the world in which at least one book of the Bible has been published since Gutenberg first printed the Bible.

We have been looking at the stages of the journey of the Bible from God to us. Since English is our mother tongue, our focus in this last chapter is on the translation and production of English editions of the Bible. We will first look at the main early ancient versions, then the first English versions up to the King James Version. With that background, we will survey the appearances of modern English Bibles, revised versions, and Bible study editions. This is where we are today—reading and studying in our mother tongue the Book that God sent on its way more than three thousand years ago!

But before we survey that history of versions, let's recognize the thousands of translators whom God has used. Without translators there would be no translations. What an important task the Bible translator has in the kingdom of God! He must bridge the gap between two different languages. For example, think of the translator whom we'll call Translator A, whose task is to translate the New Testament from the original Greek language into English. He has a three-fold task, as shown by the accompanying diagram.

Translator A works on answering three main questions, in this order:

1. *What were the original Greek words of the autographs?* For this, Translator A relies on the work done by specialists before his time, who have reconstructed the original text from copies of ancient manuscripts, and have published these in printed editions. The diagram includes the United Bible Societies' *Greek New Testament*, which has been a standard since 1966. This is one of the Greek editions that was used by translators in the making of modern English versions such as the New International Version (NIV).

2. *What do those Greek words mean?* Before Translator A decides on an English word for his translation, he must determine the *meaning* of the Greek word (or phrase) in its context. This is a crucial part of the task.

3. *How can that meaning be best expressed in English?* The translator's goal is a translation that is accurate, clear, and understandable. He aims at an

THE BIBLE TRANSLATOR'S TASK

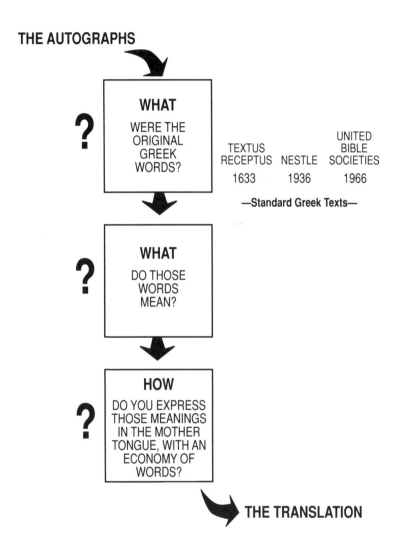

THE AUTOGRAPHS

? **WHAT** WERE THE ORIGINAL GREEK WORDS?

TEXTUS RECEPTUS	NESTLE	UNITED BIBLE SOCIETIES
1633	1936	1966

—Standard Greek Texts—

? **WHAT** DO THOSE WORDS MEAN?

? **HOW** DO YOU EXPRESS THOSE MEANINGS IN THE MOTHER TONGUE, WITH AN ECONOMY OF WORDS?

THE TRANSLATION

economy of words—that is, one English word for one Greek word, whenever possible. He uses a simple style, and avoids complicated sentences.

Here's how one publisher of a new Bible version expresses the main objectives of its translators:

> The primary concern was that the translation be accurate and faithful to the original manuscripts. . . . The second concern was to make the language simple enough for everyone to read the Bible and understand it for himself. . . . Sentences have been kept relatively short and uncomplicated. . . . For difficult words which have no simpler synonyms, footnotes and dictionary references are provided.[17]

The completed translation made by Translator A is called a *primary version*. It is called *primary* because the translation (English) is just one step from the original language (Greek). On the worldwide scene today, most Bible translators are of the *secondary* type. When Translator B translates the English version into another language, such as Papuan, that Papuan New Testament is called a *secondary version* (two steps away from the original language). The title *secondary* does not imply lesser accuracy than *primary*, because Translator B, though not a specialist in the original language, is highly trained in the use of related sources and methods of translation.

I. Early Ancient Translations

We will have a deeper appreciation for the English Bible in our hands if we know some of the highlights along the translation road. So let's spend a little time learning the story of translated Bible versions. That story begins in ancient times, in the years before Christ.

A. *The Greek Septuagint.* The first translation ever made of Scripture was this Greek Old Testament, which we first learned about in an earlier chapter. Alexandrian Jews of Egypt translated the first five books (Pentateuch) of the Old Testament in 280 B.C. They translated all the Old Testament by 180 B.C. We know that Jesus liked this Greek translation—really a "modern" version in his day—because some of his quotes of the Old Testament are from that version.

One important value of the Septuagint was that the New Testament writers then had a Greek theological vocabulary to work with when they later wrote their Greek New Testament books.

Also, the Septuagint had a missionary function: it made the Old Testament revelation accessible to the Gentile world. When the Greek New Testament was complete, Septuagint Old Testament and Greek New Testament came together as a unit—the whole Bible. So the Septuagint prepared the soil of the world for the gospel seed.

Some Christians today object to modern versions because the new versions translate some words of the traditional King James Bible text by modern words. The problem is understandable, but the solution is found in adjustment. For example, when Paul wrote about the Jews' sacred *Torah* (Law), as in Romans 2:17, he may have hesitated a little as he wrote *Nomos*—the Greek Septuagint version's word for Law—instead of the Hebrew word *Torah*. But he wrote *Nomos* nevertheless. The Septuagint had prepared the Jews, including Paul, for this language adjustment. The Septuagint version represents the first time in history that people had to adjust to a new version of the Bible. And Jesus was willing to make that adjustment: he quoted from the Hebrew Old Testament, *and he also* quoted from the Greek translation of that Scripture!

Finally, the Septuagint was the basis for the important Latin Vulgate version. This was the Bible of Christendom for one thousand years.

B. *Translation and the early church.* Jesus' last commission to his followers was to "go and make disciples of all nations" (Matthew 28:19, NIV). Before Jesus ascended into heaven from the Mount of Olives, he told his disciples specifically that the witness of the gospel should keep on multiplying to lands beyond: "You will be my witnesses—in Jerusalem, in all of Judea, in Samaria, and in every part of the world" (Acts 1:8). During the centuries after Jesus ascended, the disciples and local churches obeyed the commission and preached the gospel in all those lands. As groups of believers kept growing in these "foreign" lands, the Spirit of God moved in their hearts to get the Scriptures translated into their mother tongues. Look at the accompanying map and locate Jerusalem, which is shown as a star (*). Observe how the divinely-directed translation project kept expanding into distant lands. Note the location of Britain on the map (the "Anglo-Saxon" version), and don't lose sight of the fact that *your English Bible* came out of *that* setting.

As you read the next pages, keep in mind that the grand purpose of all translations is to open the door of communication from God to the people of his creation. Remember, that communication is where the journey of the Bible to *you* began!

C. *Latin Bible.* The Latin version of the Bible is important in the Bible's journey for various reasons, including these three:

1. It was the Bible of Christendom for one thousand years.
2. It was the first Bible introduced to the people of the British Isles.
3. The first English Bible was translated from it.

This Latin Bible (called Vulgate, meaning "common") originated during the second or third century A.D. in North Africa. Latin was the official language of much of the population there. In A.D. 383 Pope Damasus commissioned a scholar named Jerome to revise the old edition of that Latin translation. Jerome completed the whole Bible

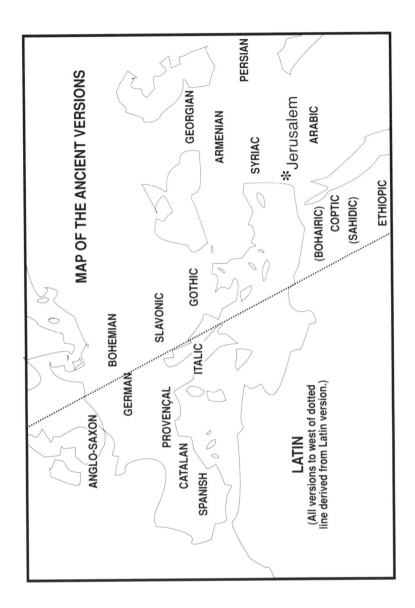

MAP OF THE ANCIENT VERSIONS

PERSIAN

GEORGIAN

ARMENIAN

SYRIAC

*Jerusalem

ARABIC

(BOHAIRIC)

COPTIC

(SAHIDIC)

ETHIOPIC

BOHEMIAN

SLAVONIC

GOTHIC

GERMAN

ITALIC

ANGLO-SAXON

PROVENÇAL

CATALAN

SPANISH

LATIN
(All versions to west of dotted
line derived from Latin version.)

by 405. The revised version became the official Bible of
the western church. The Douay Version, translated from
the Vulgate, is the authorized English Roman Catholic
Bible today.

D. *Other early versions.* During the early centuries after Christ, many new Bible versions appeared in different countries. Look again at the versions on the map. Some of the approximate dates of those versions are:

Syriac (second century)
Egyptian-Coptic (second or third century)
Gothic (A.D. 350)
Armenian (A.D. 400)
Georgian (fifth century)
Ethiopic (A.D. 600)
Arabic (seventh century)
Slavonic (A.D. 870)

When the gospel was preached in western Europe, the Latin Vulgate was the preacher's Bible. Laymen of the various countries involved sought to have the Bible translated into their mother tongues, and this brought about Bibles in their languages, translated from the Latin. Notice on the map the countries of western Europe where these Latin-based translations were made: Italic, Provencal, Catalan, Spanish, German, and Anglo-Saxon.

II. English Versions Leading to the King James Version

To learn about the first Bibles translated into English, we must turn to the early history of the British Isles. Christianity was planted in Britain by the beginning of the fourth century, but Latin was the people's language at that time. It wasn't until the fifth century, with the arrival of Germanic-speaking Angles and Saxons and Jutes, that a new language mix was becoming the people's vocabulary and grammar. That was the first of three periods of the English language, now called by these names: Old English, Middle English, and New English. Let's look at the translation activity of those periods:

A. *Old English* **(A.D. 400-1100).** We know of only a few English Bible translations made during this time. Most of the Bible translators were clergymen, who made either literal translations or paraphrases of various parts of Scripture. The best-known of these translators was the godly monk and teacher, Bede, of north England. He translated the Gospel of John around A.D. 735.

B. *Middle English* **(A.D. 1100-1520).** Translation activity during these centuries was minimal. Richard Rolle translated Psalms and parts of the New Testament, into a dialect of Middle English. The famous name of this period is John Wycliffe (d. 1384), whose labors helped bring about the first translation of the entire Bible into English.

C. *New English* **(A.D. 1520-present).** Between the Middle English and New English periods three things happened that made the years of the New English period so fruitful:

1. A revival of learning increased the knowledge of Hebrew and Greek, enabling Bible translators to read the original languages more accurately.

2. The invention of the printing press (1456) increased the circulation of Bibles immeasurably.

3. There was great interest in translating Scripture into the people's vernacular from the original language. Luther's German New Testament (1522) was the pioneer version with laymen in mind.
Below are listed some of the most important English versions of the early years of the New English period, before the King James Version:

a. *Tyndale's versions* **(1525-1535)**—New Testament and parts of the Old Testament.

b. *Coverdale's Bible* (1535)—the first printed English Bible; also the first Bible to introduce chapter summaries before each chapter, as a help to the Bible reader.

c. *Matthew's Bible* (1537) and Taverner's Bible (1539).

d. *Great Bible* (1539)—revision of Matthew's Bible, done by Coverdale.

4. Then in 1560 and 1568 two revisions of the Great Bible appeared, which were soon to bring about the King James Version in an unanticipated way. The two revised versions were the Geneva Bible and Bishops' Bible.

a. *Geneva Bible* (1560). This version was done by reformers who had fled to Geneva, Switzerland. Their translation excelled in accuracy, but they made the mistake of including notes in the margins of the pages. The notes reflected their theological viewpoint, which was a Reformed Calvinistic interpretation. This Geneva Bible was the first edition to print each verse as a paragraph, and to print in italics words not in the original texts.

b. *Bishops' Bible* (1568). This was also a revision of the Great Bible. It was made by English bishops to counter the Calvinistic Geneva edition. It promoted the British Anglican theology in its margins. Now there were two main Bibles in the British Isles, competing for leadership as *the people's Bible*. This was the background for the appearance of the *King James Version*.

5. *The King James Version* (1611). The rivalry of the two Bibles mentioned above, Geneva and Bishops',

was too big to be ignored, because it was widening the rift between the two main theological camps of England, Reformed and Anglican. In 1604 King James called together the Hampton Court Conference to discuss the views of the rival parties in the Church of England. One leader at the conference recommended making a new translation that would not propagate in its margins either theological viewpoint, Reformed or Anglican. King James favored the suggestion, and appointed fifty-four scholars to do the work. Seven years later the King James Version (KJV—also called the Authorized Version) joined the ranks of translated Bibles. Within ten years' time it became the most popular English Bible, and has stayed on this level of circulation ever since.

That decision of King James was one of the high points in the history of the Christian world. F. F. Bruce says:

> It meant in the sequel that all the non-Roman English-speaking world received one and the same English Bible as a common heritage. It is not the Bible of high church or low church, state church or free church, Episcopalian, Presbyterian or Independent, Baptist or Paedobaptist, Briton or American; it has remained The Bible *par excellence* wherever the English tongue is spoken for over three hundred years.[18]

And when we keep in mind that the publishing of many new excellent Bibles in recent years has not diminished the popularity of the King James Version, we have to conclude that it came to the world and remains in the world for a unique ministry. The story of the King James Version is a big part of the journey of the Bible from God to the world. In the words of one writer:

> There are excellent newer translations. But in 350 years no Bible has surpassed the King James Version in popularity, in literary beauty, or in its impact on the life of English-speaking peoples.[19]

III. Later English Versions

Eventually, the time came when the English-speaking church saw the need to revise the King James Version. Four of the reasons for revision were: (1) to make the text more understandable; (2) changes in the English language—some words changing meaning, and some becoming obsolete; (3) new discoveries of ancient manuscripts; and (4) increased knowledge of the Bible languages, Hebrew, Aramaic, and Greek.

The King James Version was 259 years old when a Revision Committee of Convocation was formed in England in 1870 to revise its text. While translators worked on the project in England, a group in America did the same, using an American shade of English vocabulary. The two groups worked at the same time on both sides of the ocean, and shared their work as the projects moved along. Finally, the English Revised Version (ERV) was published in 1881-1885, and the American Standard Version (ASV) appeared soon after, in 1901. This was the beginning of the twentieth century, and it is interesting to observe how many English Bible versions appeared in the decades that followed. The accompanying list identifies some of the major English Bible versions of the twentieth century, up to 1988. The list shows a larger number of versions appearing in the decades after World War II (fifties, sixties, and seventies). Also included in the list are some study Bibles which offer many aids for studying whichever Bible text is used.

A. *1881-1937*. These were the opening decades of modern English Bible translations.

1. English Revised Version, (ERV, 1881). British revision of King James Version.

2. American Standard Version, (ASV, 1901). American revision of King James Version.

3. New Testament in Modern English, (1903), R. F. Weymouth. Text is arranged in paragraphs, with chapter and verse divisions in the margins.

4. New Translation of the Bible, (1913, 1924), James Moffatt. The language has been called "fresh and colorful."

5. The Complete Bible: An American Translation, (1927, New Testament), E. J. Goodspeed. Goodspeed wanted this to be "an American translation for American readers" in their own vernacular.

6. Williams' New Testament, (1937), Charles B. Williams. Translation emphasizes the tenses of the Greek verbs.

7. Study editions of the KJV text:

> **a. Scofield Reference Bible**, (1909). This study Bible has commentary notes by C. E. Scofield.

> **b. The Thompson Chain Reference Bible**, (1934). This edition has a large variety of study aids. Two of four columns on each page of the Bible text are filled with word and verse references for comparison with other parts of the Bible.

B. *1940s*

1. Berkeley, (1945). Short helpful notes appear at times. New Testament translated by Gerrit Verkuyl. Old Testament done by twenty translators. See MLB, 1959.

2. Revised Standard Version, (RSV, 1946, New Testament). Revision of American Standard Version by the International Council of Religious Education.

C. *1950s*

1. Revised Standard Version, (RSV, 1952). Revision of American Standard Version.

2. A New Testament in Plain English, (1952). C. K. Williams.

3. Kenneth S. Wuest (New Testament), (1956-1959). An expanded translation.

4. J. B. Phillips (New Testament), (1958). Free paraphrase.

5. The Amplified New Testament, (1958). Word meanings, rather than flowing sentences, is the format. Technically, it is not a translation.

6. The Modern Language Bible, (MLB, 1959). This was the new name given to the Berkeley New Testament, when the Old Testament came together with the New Testament.

D. *1960s*

1. New English Bible, (NEB, New Testament, 1961). By British translators.

2. New American Standard Bible, (NASB, New Testament, 1963). Revision of American Standard Version, under conservative, evangelical auspices.

3. The Amplified Bible, (TAB, 1965).

4. Today's English Version, (TEV, New Testament, 1966). A very readable translation. Another name of the version: *Good News for Modern Man*.

5. The Living Bible, (TLB, New Testament, 1966). Paraphrased text by Ken Taylor. Paraphrases are very free.

6. Jerusalem Bible, (JB, 1966). Catholic version. A respected translation from Hebrew and Greek (not from the Latin Vulgate).

E. *1970s*

1. New American Bible, (NAB, Old Testament and New Testament, 1970). Catholic version.

2. New English Bible, (NEB, 1970). British version.

3. New American Standard Bible, (NASB, 1971).

4. The Living Bible, (TLB, 1971).

5. New International Version, (NIV, New Testament, 1973). By evangelical translators.

6. Today's English Version, (TEV, 1976).

7. Ryrie's Study Bible, (1976 ff.) Available in these texts: NKJV, NASB, NIV.

8. New International Version, (NIV, 1978). This is the best selling English Bible translation in some parts of the world. In the first ten years, over fifty million copies were distributed.

F. *1980s*

1. New King James Bible, (NKJV, 1982). Revision of King James Version.

2. Narrated Bible, (1984). The entire Bible text is printed in chronological order.

3. New International Version Study Bible, (1985). Extensive background and study notes, with many maps and charts.

4. The Everyday Bible, (TEB, 1987). Excellent edition of the *New Century Version* (1986). Wording of the text is clear and sharp, simple enough for all ages to read and understand. There is a Special New Testament Study Edition of TEB, which has two-page introductions and study helps for each New Testament book.

The above list of selected English Bible versions and Study Bibles shows how blessed we are today with such a variety of choices, to fill our needs and likes for reading and studying the Bible. A visit to a Christian bookstore or a look at a publisher's catalog can be a happy, exciting experience!

IV. Literal or Free Translations?

One of the most important decisions we make when choosing a Bible version for reading and study concerns how literal a translation it is. Each Bible is one of three kinds of translation: literal, free, or very free (paraphrase).

A. *Literal Translation.* A literal translation stresses faithfulness to the original Hebrew and Greek texts, to preserve the original flavor intended by the author. The translator seeks to translate each Hebrew or Greek word by one English word, as much as possible. This is known as "economy of words." Literal translations may be rigid and unclear in places. Their special value is that they preserve the quantity and exactness of the original author's vocabulary. The text itself, not the translator's interpretation, is preserved intact.

B. *Free Translation.* The main objective of a free translation or paraphrase (very free) is to keep the text on the reader's plane so that he or she can understand it. The translator is not limited by the number or kinds of words in expressing the *meaning* of the original text. The differences between paraphrases and free translations, as used here, is that paraphrases go to greater extremes to give shades of meaning to the Bible text. In a paraphrase such as *The Living Bible* (TLB), the translator often uses modern-day idioms. The value of the paraphrase is its clarity and attempt to explain difficult words and phrases. Its weakness is that the translator is giving his own interpretation, which may be misleading at times.

The chart on the following page shows a list of some major, modern English Bible versions, the order of the list going from the very literal NKJV, to the very paraphrastic TLB. Remember that no version is 100 percent paraphrastic or 100 percent literal. A paraphrase is *mainly* paraphrastic. A free translation is *mainly* free. And a literal translation is *mainly* literal. When we read on pages 114 to 117 the text of Romans 15:1-4 as it is published in each of eleven versions, we can see how the versions teach the same truths in different ways and with different shades of the English language.

God is in the picture of the different kinds of translations described above. That is because God wants the Good News to reach *all* people in the most effective way. A Bible *paraphrase* may be the best first version for a nonbeliever to read, to learn about Christ and the way of salvation. An earnest Christian who has been growing in the Lord may gain a deeper understanding of the Bible by spending most of his or her study time slowly analyzing the Bible text of a *literal* translation. It will be very helpful to compare the paraphrase Bible while analyzing a literal translation.

(NKJV, 1982)	**literal translations**	1. NEW KING JAMES VERSION
(NASB, 1971)		2. NEW AMERICAN STANDARD BIBLE
(RSV, 1952)		3. REVISED STANDARD VERSION
(MLB, 1959)	**to**	4. MODERN LANGUAGE BIBLE (Berkeley)
(NIV, 1978)		5. NEW INTERNATIONAL VERSION
(TEB, 1987)	**free translations**	6. THE EVERYDAY BIBLE
(TEV, 1976)		7. TODAY'S ENGLISH VERSION
(NEB, 1970)		8. NEW ENGLISH BIBLE
(JB, 1966)	**to**	9. JERUSALEM BIBLE
(PHILLIPS, 1958)		10. NEW TESTAMENT IN MODERN ENGLISH
(TLB, 1971)	**paraphrases**	11. THE LIVING BIBLE

READINGS OF ROMANS 15:1-4 IN ELEVEN VERSIONS

(The order moves from the most literal, NKJV, to the most paraphrastic, TLB.)

(1) *New King James Version* (NKJV)

1 WE then who are strong ought to bear with the scruples of the weak, and not to please ourselves. 2 Let each of us please *his* neighbor for *his* good, leading to edification. 3 For even Christ did not please Himself; but as it is written, *"The reproaches of those who reproached You fell on Me."* 4 For whatever things were written before were written for our learning, that we through the patience and comfort of the Scriptures might have hope.

(2) *New American Standard Bible* (NASB)

1 NOW we who are strong ought to bear the weaknesses of those without strength and not *just* please ourselves. 2 Let each of us please his neighbor for his good, to his edification. 3 For even Christ did not please Himself, but as it is written "THE REPROACHES OF THOSE WHO REPROACHED THEE FELL UPON ME." 4 For whatever was written in earlier times was written for our instruction, that through perseverance and the encouragement of the Scriptures we might have hope.

(3) *Revised Standard Version* (RSV)

1 We who are strong ought to bear with the failings of the weak, and not to please ourselves; 2 let each of us please his neighbor for his good, to edify him. 3 For Christ did not please himself; but, as it is written, "The reproaches of those who reproached thee fell on me." 4 For whatever was written in former days was written for our instruction, that by steadfastness and by the encouragement of the scriptures we might have hope.

(4) *Modern Language Bible* (MLB), Berkeley Version

1 WE WHO ARE STRONG OUGHT TO bear with the scruples of those who are weak. We should not please ourselves. 2 But each of us should please his neighbor for his welfare, to strengthen him. 3 For even Christ did not please Himself but, as it is written, "The reproaches of those who reproached you fell on me." 4 All those writings of long ago were written for our instruction, so that through the patience and encouragement of the Scriptures we might have hope.

(5) *New International Version* (NIV)

1 We who are strong ought to bear with the failings of the weak and not to please ourselves. 2 Each of us should please his neighbor for his good, to build him up. 3 For even Christ did not please himself but, as it is written: "The insults of those who insult you have fallen on me." 4 For everything that was written in the past was written to teach us, so that through endurance and the encouragement of the Scriptures we might have hope.

(6) *The Everyday Bible* (TEB)

1 We who are strong in faith should help those who are weak. We should help them with their weaknesses, and not please only ourselves. 2 Let each of us please his neighbor for his good, to help him be stronger in faith. 3 Even Christ did not live to please himself. It was as the Scriptures said: "When people insult you, it hurts me." 4 Everything that was written in the past was written to teach us, so that we could have hope. That hope comes from the patience and encouragement that the Scriptures give us.

(7) *Today's English Version* (TEV)—Good News for Modern Man

1 We who are strong in the faith ought to help the weak to carry their burdens. We should not please ourselves. 2 Instead, we should all please our brothers for their own good, in order to build them up in the faith. 3 For Christ did not please himself. Instead, as the scripture says, "The insults which are hurled at you have fallen on me." 4 Everything written in the Scriptures was written to teach us, in order that we might have hope through the patience and encouragement which the Scriptures give us.

(8) *New English Bible* (NEB)

1 Those of us who have a robust conscience must accept as our own burden the tender scruples of weaker men, and not consider ourselves. 2 Each of us must consider his neighbor and think what is for his good and will build up the common life. 3 For Christ too did not consider himself, but might have said, in the words of Scripture, 'The reproaches of those who reproached thee fell upon me.' 4 For all the ancient scriptures were written for our own instruction, in order that through the encouragement they give us we may maintain our hope with fortitude.

(9) *Jerusalem Bible* (JB)

1 We who are strong have a duty to put up the qualms of the weak without thinking of ourselves. 2 Each of us should think of his neighbors and help them to become stronger Christians. 3 Christ did not think of himself: the words of scripture—*the insults of those who insult you fall on me*—apply to him. 4 And indeed everything that was written long ago in the scriptures was meant to teach us something about

hope from the examples scripture gives of how people who did not give up were helped by God.

(10) *New Testament in Modern English* (Phillips)

1 We who have strong faith ought to shoulder the burden of the doubts and qualms of others and not just to go our own sweet way. 2 Our actions should mean the good of others—should help them to build up their characters. 3 For even Christ did not choose his own pleasure, but as it is written:

The reproaches of them that reproached thee fell upon me.

4 For all those words which were written long ago are meant to teach us today; that when we read in the scriptures of the endurance of men and of all the help that God gave them in those days, we may be encouraged to go on hoping in our time.

(11) *The Living Bible* (TLB)

1 Even if we believe that it makes no difference to the Lord whether we do these things, still we cannot just go ahead and do them to please ourselves; for we must bear the "burden" of being considerate of the doubts and fears of others—of those who feel these things are wrong. 2 Let's please the other fellow, not ourselves, and do what is for his good and thus build him up in the Lord. 3 Christ didn't please himself. As the Psalmist said, "He came for the very purpose of suffering under the insults of those who were against the Lord." 4 These things that were written in the Scriptures so long ago are to teach us patience and to encourage us, so that we will look forward expectantly to the time when God will conquer sin and death.

V. Study Bibles Today

Bible study and prayer are two of the most important activities of Christian living. When we're studying the Bible, we are carefully and prayerfully listening to God speak to us. The Bible is God's written Word to us. It is the message He has wanted to communicate. The Bible is the book God sent on its journey to us thousands of years ago. He wants us to study it diligently.

In the introduction of this book I described how, as a teenager, I was introduced to a study Bible for the first time. A whole new world seemed to open up before me because I saw the pages of the Bible in a new light. The Bible text seemed to want to talk. And I wanted to respond in the margin with a pencil. I would get personally involved in examining not only the individual lines of the Bible text, but also the connections between lines and phrases and words. No word was an orphan, and it seemed like the groups of words were in happy fellowship, proclaiming the Good News of God.

I began to use a pencil every time I studied a Bible passage. I marked the Bible text to show key truths. My study Bible had many blank spaces in the margins for my notations. I soon began to see that it was important for me to observe not only *what* the Bible author wrote, but *how* he wrote it. This was only natural, since the Bible is *God talking to us*, and God never speaks in a monotone.

Some years later, when I was introduced to the inductive method of Bible study, I began printing the Bible text on paper, phrase by phrase, letting the text talk in the way the author was composing it. If he emphasized a word or phrase strongly, I might print it with larger letters, or underline it. I could make my "textual re-creation" show connections between words and phrases by using a few lines and similar print. My printing and markings might show repetitions, and contrasts, and progressions, and even pauses. All in all, I was letting the Bible text talk, which is why I eventually referred to it as a "talking text".[20] Little did I know what a large part the talking text would play in my own personal Bible study in the years to come.

So the first day I used my own copy of the study Bible was truly a milestone in my Christian experience. From that day on, Bible study would always be exciting and enjoyable, inspiring and challenging.

Study Bibles appeared on the publishing scene in the early decades of this century, but the eighties have been *the* decade of study Bibles. More and more, Christians have wanted not only to *read* the Bible, but also to get excited about studying it—hence the new editions of the Bible that are geared to the student, with many different kinds of study aids.

The best study Bibles print the Bible text paragraph by paragraph, and show groups of paragraphs[21] by outline headings. Two Bibles arranged that way are the *New International Version Study Bible* and *The Everyday Bible*. The New Testament edition of *The Everyday Bible*, called *Special New Testament Study Edition* (1988),[22] has helpful guides and instructions that show the reader how to study the Bible text for himself or herself. Its objective is to make Bible study effective and enjoyable. The format of its Bible text is that of segment units (an example is John 1:1-18) broken down into paragraphs (e.g., John 1:1-5; 6-9; 10-13; 14-15; 16-18). This author considers the segment-paragraph layout of the Bible text to be the best help for analyzing a unit of the Bible.

The *Life Application Bible* (Tyndale House, 1988) gives study helps that are geared mainly to application of the Bible text. The Bible text is TLB. Among other Study Bibles that have appeared in this decade are the *Disciple's Study Bible* (NIV) (Holman, 1988); the *New Scofield Study Bible* (NKJV) (Nelson, 1989); and the *Discovery Bible New Testament* (NASB) (Moody, 1987).

Study Bibles differ as to size, depending on how many aids the editors want to include. For example, the *New International Version Study Bible* includes these study helps: introduction and outlines, study notes, cross-references, parallel passages, concordance, maps, charts, diagrams, essays, and indexes. The more they include, the smaller the print, which is one of their weaknesses.

Studying the Bible text with the aid of a study Bible can become the most exciting and profitable spiritual exercise you have ever had.

Conclusion

What a wonderful, action-packed journey this has been! When we think back over the routes the journey has followed, everything keeps pointing to the heart of God, who is Light and who is Love. God had a message he wanted to share with all people. He intended that everyone read and understand that message. The message was his Word about two great subjects: The *way to God*, and the *walk with God*. The Bible clearly shows the unsaved person the way to God, which is through faith in Jesus Christ. When he or she becomes a Christian, the rest of a lifetime can be spent reading and studying the whole Bible, learning how to walk with God, experiencing endless blessings of fellowship with him.

The whole Christian world is actively engaged in teaching, preaching, and reaching the hearts of unsaved and saved alike, through the one great Book of God. The Bible is central in these kinds of ministries:

(1) in schools: Bible institutes, Bible colleges, Christian liberal arts colleges, Bible-centered seminaries,

Christian day schools, home schools, Sunday schools, weekday Bible study groups

(2) in families: leadership, guidance, and example of parents

(3) in churches: nurture, evangelism, missions, testimony, Christian education, programs for children, youth, and adults

(4) in para-church organizations: InterVarsity, Campus Crusade for Christ, Young Life, Walk Through the Bible, summer Bible conferences and camps, television, radio

(5) in the publishing world: books, magazines, tracts, Bible versions, study Bibles, Bible translations, self-study guides.

One of the happiest, most moving, scenes in God's view must be an individual reading and studying the pages of the Book that God sent him. It's no wonder that scribes, translators, editors, and publishers have always considered it a grand privilege to help spread the Word which God inspired his servants to write!

Only God knows the course of history in the days and years ahead. The journey of the Bible is not over, and God has his plans for the pathways of that journey yet to be. God continues to speak to us through the once-for-all message of his Book. Shouldn't the very thought of this excite and alert us to hear what he has to say?

We know God sent the Bible to us, but *have we returned thanks*? And if we have, do we show our gratitude by reading and heeding the message he sent? On the next pages, you will read about a dear old man who one day showed me the powerful force of a *grateful spirit*.

Message From the Skies

I will never forget what I learned about gratitude at the end of World War II from an elderly Norwegian. The place was Gardemoen Airfield, north of Oslo, where I served with the U.S. Air Force as a meteorologist.

I was drawing a weather map in our forecast office. There was a soft knock on the door, and an old man slowly entered, carrying a brown package. He hesitated a little, I guess because he wondered if he could communicate with me in the Norwegian language. He chose to try his English, and he did well. (I was happy for his choice, since I didn't know much Norwegian.) After we exchanged names, I invited him to sit down.

"Vaer sa god" ("Be so good").

"And where are you from?" I asked.

He said he lived in Bodø, a small Norwegian village just north of the Arctic Circle. He pointed to it on the map on our wall.

"So far away!" I exclaimed.

"Ya, ya, it is very far. It took me long to get here." He paused; then, "And I came alone."

I gathered that he had come to our weather office for a

specific purpose. I didn't want to ask him why he came. I could tell he felt he was on a mission, and I wanted him to feel free to announce it in his own way and time.

"I came to bring you this," he said, as he reached into his package and pulled out a white 8- by 8- by 4-inch plastic container. "I found this thing in the fields, far from our house. I read what it said, so here it is." Another pause, as he looked into my eyes. "And I also came to thank your country for helping my people from the invader."

I was not surprised to see that his white "thing" was one of our small radiosonde transmitters. Our weather station sent four of these into the upper atmosphere every day, to measure upper air temperature, pressure, and moisture. (We got wind data by tracking the radiosonde with radar.)

"Oh yes," I said, "a radiosonde—we sent this up into the skies, and it returned to earth—in your field!"

He seemed relieved that he had come to the right place. "The box told me to bring it here." With trembling index finger, he pointed to the words printed on the container. I read them out loud, to reinforce my commendation of his mission. This was the printed message:

NOTICE TO FINDERS: This instrument belongs to the United States Government. A balloon sent up by a weather station carried it to a height of about 12 miles. The balloon burst and the instrument came down slowly on the parachute. While in the air the instrument acted as a radio broadcaster of the temperature, pressure and moisture of the air through which it passed.

The instrument may be used again. Please remove the tag from under the flap and write the information required. Mail it at any post office or post box. No stamps are needed. If found outside the United States, it may be turned in to any U. S. Army, U. S. Navy, or U. S. Weather Bureau organization. Thank you.

When I finished reading, I saw in his eyes a gleam of honor and joy. He had received a message from the United States Government "from the skies," and now he was obeying its instructions.

Our senior friend had every reason to believe that he was contributing in *some* way to the cause of the Allies. I showed him an upper air weather map I had been working on. Earlier, a staff member had recorded the simultaneous radiosonde measurements that had been sent back to earth from the skies over the Atlantic Ocean and northwest Europe. Then I showed him how such maps assisted in making flight forecasts, predicting the paths and strengths of storms, and any threats to our pilots in flight—like aircraft icing.

It wasn't hard for me to show this thoughtful Norwegian from the Arctic Circle that I was impressed by his sacrificial response to the message on the radiosonde box. Here was an elderly man—in his eighties at least—making a long trip alone, because he wanted to help an allied nation and thank its people for defending his country. He didn't know the value of the instrument. He didn't know specifically how it helped the weather station. He didn't know how (and whether) it might be used again. But what he *did* know was that the instrument belonged to the United States, who was asking any finder to return it. He was a finder, and he wanted to obey the instructions and also say "Thanks."

We visited for a little while, talking about his family in Bodø and my own relatives in southern Norway. Then he rose from his chair, and we said good-bye. I couldn't help but think how happy his return trip would be, with the contented spirit of a grateful and obedient heart.

What about the message the Lord sent us "from the skies," in the pages of his great Book? How grateful are we? He has told us how to be saved, and how to live the Christian life. Have we thanked him for sending us that matchless message of eternal life? Are we reading the Book, and obeying its instructions? Or is he having to say, to our shame, "Why do you call me 'Lord, Lord,' but do not do what I say?" (Luke 6:46).

Notes

1. Gleason L. Archer, *A Survey of Old Testament Introduction* (Chicago: Moody Press, 1964), 21 (emphasis added).

2. Klaas Runia, "The Modern Debate Around the Bible," *Christianity Today* (August 16, 1968), 8.

3. To understand this scholarly usage of the word *autograph*, think of it this way: The "autograph" of a Bible book is the very first copy—the one on which the human author would have signed his autograph!

4. D. Lee Chestnut, *The Atom Speaks* (Grand Rapids, Mich.: Eerdmans, 1951), 64.

5. Robert Mounce, "Is the New Testament Historically Accurate?" in *Can I Trust My Bible?* (Chicago: Moody Press, 1963), 174.

6. William F. Albright, "Return to Biblical Theology," *The Christian Century* (November 19, 1958), 1328.

7. Kenneth S. Kantzer, "Inspiration," Merrill C. Tenney (ed.), *The Zondervan Pictorial Bible Dictionary* (Grand Rapids, Mich.: Zondervan Publishing House, 1963), 380.

8. "Chicago Statement on Biblical Inerrancy," (International Council on Biblical Inerrancy, Chicago Conference, 1978).

9. Edward J. Young, *An Introduction to the Old Testament* (Grand Rapids, Mich.: Eerdmans, 1949), 10–11.

10. F. F. Bruce, *The Books and the Parchments,* rev. (Old Tappan, N.J.: Fleming H. Revell Co., 1984), 161.

11. Chart from Irving L. Jensen, *Galatians* (Chicago: Moody Press, 1973), 8.

12. F. J. Foakes-Jackson, quoted by F. F. Bruce, *The Books and the Parchments*, 104.

13. Quoted by Philip Schaff, ed., in *The Nicene and Post-Nicene Fathers*, 2d series, vol. 1 (Grand Rapids, Mich.: Eerdmans, 1952), 549.

14. Philip Schaff, *Companion to the Greek Testament and the English Version* (New York: Harper & Row, 1883), 177.

15. G. Douglas Young, *The Evangelical Beacon* (April 7, 1959), 7.

16. Frederic G. Kenyon, quoted in Norman L. Geisler and William E. Nix, *A General Introduction to the Bible* (Chicago: Moody Press, 1968), 248.

17. *The Everyday Bible: Special New Testament Study Edition*, (Minneapolis: World Wide Publications, 1988), 7.

18. F. F. Bruce, *The Books and the Parchments*, 220.

19. Don Wharton, "The Greatest Bible of Them All," *Reader's Digest* (December, 1961), 103.

20. For examples of "talking text," see Irving L. Jensen, *Do-It-Yourself Bible Studies* (San Bernardino: Here's Life Publishers, 1983 to 1990), which print a talking text of each Bible passage being studied.

21. A group of paragraphs is a unit of study called a segment. Bible study segments, supported by talking text, is in the format of my *Bible Self-Study Guides*, new edition (Chicago: Moody Press, 1990).

22. *The Everyday Bible: Special New Testament Study Edition* (Minneapolis: World Wide Publications, 1988).

Selected Bibliography

Barnard, Richard Kevin. *God's Word in Our Language*. Colorado Springs: International Bible Society, 1989.

Bruce, F. F. *The Books and the Parchments*. Rev. ed. Old Tappan, N. J.: Fleming H. Revell, 1984. Highly recommended.

_____. *The English Bible: A History of Translations*. New rev. ed. New York: Oxford University, 1970.

_____. *The New Testament Documents: Are They Reliable?* Grand Rapids, Mich.: Eerdmans, 1965.

Burrows, Millar. *More Light on the Dead Sea Scrolls*. New York: Viking, 1958.

Can I Trust My Bible? Chicago: Moody, 1963.

Geisler, Norman L., and William E. Nix. *A General Introduction to the Bible*. Rev. ed. Chicago: Moody, 1968.

Grant, Frederick C. *Translating the Bible*. Greenwich, Conn.: Seabury, 1961.

Harris, R. Laird. *Inspiration and Canonicity of the Bible*. Grand Rapids, Mich.: Zondervan, 1957.

Kubo, Sakae, and Walter Specht. *So Many Versions?* Grand Rapids, Mich.: Zondervan, 1975.

MacGregor, Geddes. *The Bible in the Making*. New York: J. B. Lippincott, 1959.

Orr, James. *Revelation and Inspiration*. Grand Rapids, Mich.: Eerdmans, 1952.

Reumann, John. *The Romance of Bible Scripts and Scholars*. Englewood Cliffs, N.J.: Prentice Hall, 1965.

Weigle, Luther A. *The English New Testament from Tyndale to the Revised Standard Version*. New York: Abingdon-Cokesbury, 1949.